Culture Detox 2
Celebrating Self not Celebrity

Dr Carla Cornelius

Jesus Joy Publishing

First Published and printed in Great Britain in 2021 by
Jesus Joy Publishing, a division of Eklegein Ltd.

Scripture Quotations

ISBN 978-1-90797-167-9

Jesus Joy Publishing
A division of Eklegein Ltd
www.jesusjoypublishing.co.uk
250321

Dedication

To those who, like me, sought refuge from the uncomfortable realities of this life, by escaping into celebrity culture. You may not have realised that you were masking more fundamental needs. In sharing my epiphanies, it is my hope that you will experience epiphanies of your own

To those who feel powerless to detach from the popular culture's all-pervasive grip. It is my prayer that this book will help to set you free.

Acknowledgements

A debt of gratitude is owed to my beloved parents, Richard and Hazel Cheltenham, for instilling in me from a young age a love of learning and an interest in people. As readers themselves, our home was always well stocked with a variety of books – 'a bookworm's paradise'.

I continue to be humbled and inspired by my precious son, whose challenges redirected me to my path of destiny, and who keeps me grounded and focused on this narrow path.

Last but not least, there are no words to adequately express my appreciation to my amazing husband, Michael, who helped me to realise my dream to become a published author. His feedback and encouragement have been invaluable in the production of this book, and every book so far. I hope and pray God will grant us the opportunity to birth more 'brainchildren' together.

Contents

Foreword: My Story

This book has been birthed from a personal awakening. Like so many, I have spent most of my life so far feeding on pop culture. This was not a sudden epiphany. As touched on in the first book in this series, I grew up on the pop culture staple of American TV . Our worst habits are often formed in childhood, and threaten to keep us in their grip throughout our entire lives. Even when we are well aware of the emotional, physical or financial havoc they are wreaking in our lives, we may still feel powerless to break them. We often need several wake up calls before we muster the courage to rouse ourselves from our passivity, and pursue a different path.

It was no co-incidence I was drawn to strong female characters on screen. This is a natural part of the psychology of early child development – a need to find mentors to whom to aspire. It never occurred to me that they were eligible female mentors right under my nose in my family and community. It didn't dawn on me that my on-screen idols were the products of the imagination of a team of show business employees, and that I too could use my imagination to create a life for myself that would be exciting and fulfilling.

Paige Matheson in 'Knots Landing' was convincingly portrayed by Nicolette Sheridan as a ruthlessly ambitious young woman. It didn't hurt that she was also physically alluring; in my head these two qualities went hand in hand, so conditioned was I by fairy tales such as 'Beauty and the Beast', 'Snow White' and 'Rapunzel' where the heroines are always beautiful.

Out of the grit and violence of downtown New York emerged the indomitable duo of 'Cagney and Lacey' whose eponymous show garnered 14 Emmy awards in seven seasons. The acting was so good that I could literally feel every ounce of Cagney's pain, not realising until I was much older, that she was an alcoholic; this accounted for the fact that her life was full of melodrama and angst. Forget dysfunction, when for 50 minutes, I could enter her superhuman mind and body as she navigated the dangers of being a detective in New York's 14th precinct. I was mesmerised by her passion for her work and her fierce independence. As a teenager struggling to find my identity, I was still trying to find my path in life, and was plagued with self-doubt. But would I really want to walk a mile in her shoes? What made for captivating drama, did not necessarily make for an ideal life.

How could I explain my penchant for probing the biographies and background of the 'stars'? I would consume women's glossy magazines whenever I could. I fell under the spell of the 'supermodels' of the eighties, such as Cindy Crawford and Karen Mulder, and was also drawn to actresses in the Golden Age of Hollywood such as Ava Gardner, Elizabeth Taylor and Katharine Hepburn. They exuded 'impossible' beauty and elegance; the characters they portrayed exuded strength and confidence. They made the lives of the women I knew look terribly dull by comparison. Indeed, they made my life seem dull by comparison.

As far as I was concerned, they had made it, so I was keen to gain some pearls of wisdom so that I could hopefully make a success of my own life. I wanted to be wise and learn from others' mistakes so that I didn't have to make them all myself. Although this reasoning seems sound, I didn't realise how flawed it was. Whilst affirming others' strengths is good, putting celebrities on a pedestal involved ignoring blatant flaws and over-inflating the positives.

By the age of 18, I already knew sub-consciously that I wanted to write books, but I did not have the confidence to admit this because on the tiny island of Barbados where I grew up, there were no role models I knew who had done so, and were making a living out of it.

After completing a first degree in law which was driven more by my parents' ambition than mine, in my early twenties I auditioned at the 'Poor School' (formerly a drama school located in London) and considered applying for a master's degree in film studies. In neither instance was I really interested in the craft of acting, but I had simply caught the fame bug. Looking back, I realise that I was desperately searching for meaning and purpose, and was relying on pop culture to define it for me. I was subconsciously defining success in terms of how many people knew my name, rather than a service to humanity.

I began to collect newspaper and magazine articles and photos of the rich and famous. I now know that at a deeper level, I wanted to be them, and live those lives so glamorously portrayed. Being myself seemed drab and unfulfilling; I had my whole life ahead of me, but I was at a loss which path to take.

As I grew older, I realised that pop culture is full of smoke and mirrors – through rose-tinted lenses, it offers a glimpse into a world which stimulates the senses and the imagination like nothing else, but all the illusions can be shattered and evaporate in an instance. I rationalised to myself that somehow being privy to their lives would inspire me to make a success of my own life. I was yet to learn a most fundamental lesson that you can never truly succeed at being someone else, only yourself. I didn't realise it at the time but like most people in their twenties, I was struggling to find out who I was, why I was here, where I belonged, and what to do with that most precious and expendable commodity – time. What I had lost over the years was not so much money, but time which could never be recovered. Even more importantly, I had lost a sense of my own significance.

When I started my Journalism course, the tutor asked the students to introduce themselves and indicate their ambitions. When my turn came, I rattled off a list of things only to be interrupted by him with the words – "that's quite a lot!" I felt snubbed, and for the rest of the week, I questioned my ambitions. Was I reaching too high? Was I deluding myself that I could be such a versatile writer, or even be a writer at all? I was yet to discover that a career is characterised by doing and not being. Therefore, to be a writer, I needed to write – plain and simple.

Later on, I was to discover that when people we look up to, don't affirm or validate our dreams but instead ignore or dismiss them, they do not magically disappear. In my case, I suppressed my dream, and tried to live out my parents' dream instead.

I was born into Barbadian culture where only certain professions were guaranteed a good income, standard of living and the respect of the community. Writing was not one of them. No-one in my family had ever earned a living as a writer. Who the heck was I to think I could break the mould? I was also drawn to Psychology, but when I mentioned it to my father, he scoffed at the notion.

Therefore, I was reluctant to challenge any further my parents' 'superior wisdom' that I should be a lawyer. I recall the day we had a Career Open Day at my secondary school, and I attended the law presentation. When my mother came to pick me up from school that afternoon, I cried. She managed to console me as best she could by encouraging me to just get the first degree under my belt. In hindsight, she was trying to breach the divide between my father's need for a successor to his law chambers, and my need to fulfil my own ambitions. She explained that the Law could be a route into other professions so it was a safe qualification to gain.

I was enrolled in a university where a two-year law degree was on offer over 4,000 miles away from home and across the Atlantic Ocean. I was being fast-tracked to my dad's law firm. By any measure, this was a 'dream job', except Law had never really been my dream. I was not prepared for life on campus – rich kids with too much money and not enough direction. Looking back now I can see that I was probably one of them. My saving grace was that I had been a high achieving student all my life, and this was all I knew how to be. I was thrown, at the deep end, into a world of students who overwhelmingly just wanted to have fun, and enjoy their freedom from parental constraints. Studying was not high on their list of priorities; this was the last place I needed to be with my pitiful lack of real enthusiasm for the Law, and a countless array of fellow students with mixed priorities.

This was where I met a particular student who was to change the course of my life forever. Because I was lacking in a strong sense of purpose in my life, I was very vulnerable to being led astray by someone who was controlling. I ended up going along with a lot that he wanted to do, and this ended up with my falling pregnant.

I decided against all logic and parental advice, but buoyed by my instincts, not to have an abortion, and my son was born. Little did I know that the same child would be the only motivating factor in my life at later points in time. He was diagnosed with autism and learning disability just before the age of three, and the train of my life which I had tried so hard to keep moving, derailed completely. It soon became clear to me that I could not continue my postgraduate studies in Law. My mind was elsewhere – it was clear that my son needed a lot of help, and I was the only one who could find it for him.

However, on the positive side, I was forced to get off the treadmill of life to look after him and rethink my future. I was forced to get out of the train and walk slowly, tentatively, towards a path of light. During this 'wilderness' experience where I felt my life had come to a standstill, I went on an inner journey of self-questioning, Bible study and prayer as I tried desperately to find my way home - to a place where I belonged - and help my son. My external world was very chaotic, but at least I was able to take a break from my own life which was lacking in true fulfilment. My son would motivate me to wake up in the morning, carry out the necessary tasks of daily living and keep on trying to make some sense of my life which was fast becoming an unbearable continuum of debt, resentment and frustration. He would also inspire me to pursue my dream to be a writer, long after his dad and I had parted ways.

Here was I – the mother of a son with cognitive deficits and what I was told was a lifelong condition. I baulked at such a prognosis, but it made me realise that I had an extraordinary gift. By contrast, I had been told all my life that I had 'unlimited' potential, yet I had been limiting myself with my own fears and self-doubt. I began to believe that I owed it, not just to myself, but to my son, to pursue my dream – because in all likelihood he would never be able to pursue his own dream, if indeed he would ever know what that was.

During this difficult period, I penned this poem which became my life anthem of sorts:

> "...I crave success, respect and recognition,
>
> to see my talents grow to fruition.

I crave that special place

under the sun -

That is uniquely my own."

[Constant Cravings]

I'm sure many of you have had a similar knock back in trying to find your purpose in life. As I stumbled towards my destiny, I would often still revert to living vicariously through the lives of those who appear to have already 'made it' or were courageously pursuing their dreams in the media limelight. I was sub-consciously hoping they would toss a few pearls of wisdom in my direction that would reveal the secrets of their successes.

I would always gravitate towards a literary biography because I told myself I was desperate to gain some insight to appropriate into my own life. After all, I reasoned, the wise person learns from others' mistakes so that she does not have to make them all herself. However, I began to realise that living vicariously through the missteps of others would not safeguard me from the risks involved in living my life and making and learning from my own mistakes. I did not feel equipped to go out into the big, wide world and live my own life. But I had to be willing to take leaps of faith into the future trusting that it would all work out in the end. Little did I realise that prying into the business of others was a way of procrastinating in my own life.

It's easy to think celebrities have it all figured out because of the applause and recognition they receive. I soon realised no other human being holds the answers to your life. Instead of chasing after celebrities, I needed to chase after God for He alone held the secrets to my life's purpose.

I began to dare myself to become *all that God created me to be*. This is not as easy as it sounds, and the journey to finding myself has not been easy, but over the years I have grown to appreciate that no-one's journey is plain sailing. My journey is still not complete, but I'm a lot farther down the road and finally learning to be patient with myself and not berate myself for too long when I stumble, and revert to habits of self-sabotage.

Note that I did not say 'become all that I can be.' In a world where conformity is king, blazing your own trail is a daunting undertaking. Nobody can tell you how to go about it simply because it has never been done before. We each have a unique place and purpose in the world. It took me the best part of thirty years to realise that I was not put on earth to fulfil others' dreams or become a carbon copy of someone else, but to become all that I was meant to be.

2004 was a major turning point my life. I met my husband-to-be and was so involved in church, family and courtship that I had no extra time to fritter away aimlessly. As a result, I was not keeping up with what was going on in the news. I didn't even recognise a particularly famous person from my homeland whose star was in the ascendancy, and someone commented at my ignorance as if I should have known this. It occurred to me in hindsight that this was how life should be – we should be more focused on what is going on in our own lives than 'breaking news' which bears no real relevance to our day-to-day lives and only serves as a talking point.

I have noticed there is something strange happening to me in recent years. I will click on the mainstream media news sites, and not recognise certain personalities in the entertainment section either by image or name. They are spoken of as if I ought to know them. The old familiar faces no longer seem to get top billing. A 'change of guard' is occurring. I feel no compelling need to become acquainted with these emerging personalities, many of whom are nearly or just over half my age. Not that they are any less talented than the 'old guard', but my interest is waning. This, I'm sure is a sign of age as much as a gaining of wisdom. I'm glad I've gained this perspective in my forties as so much time will be saved in the future not trying to keep up with celebrities. After all, 'better late than never'; plus, I'm still young enough to redirect my energies for the remainder of my life towards more worthwhile pursuits.

After a while, you just get tired of the 'merry-go-round'. What starts off as an exciting and desirable pastime, becomes a tedious and tiresome waste of time, as time goes on. I hope the readers of this book will realise that, like myself, they can get off it anytime they choose, and that a brighter path awaits them on the road of self-discovery.

Introduction

The general view is that narcissism is rife. On the contrary, the basic premise of this book is that celebrity addiction and hero worship are rife in modern societies and have led to wide scale self-neglect. We need to develop or re-learn the art of starring in our own lives as we navigate the media maelstrom of celebrity news.

One of the gods of modern living has been identified as 'entertainment'[1]. Most of those we rely on to entertain us are famous for something or the other. Not only do many worship the famous, whether it be an individual, sports team or fashion brand, but many millennials (those born between 1981 and 1996) identify their deepest longing as simply to be famous.[2]

Children between the ages of 5-10 were asked what they wanted to be when they grew up, and the top two responses were "to be rich"(22%) and "to be famous" (19%) with 6% not wanting to work at all.[3] The desire to contribute something useful and significant to society, is no longer entrenched in the value system of the culture.

Very often this desire for fame is framed in terms of 'I want to be like...' instead of asking ourselves the question – 'What is it about me that I could develop into a marketable skill?' Each of us is by definition unique, but we act as if we are ashamed of our uniqueness. We want to look, dress and have the same ambitions as those whom the media affirms are worthy of our admiration. Yet, any attempt to be someone we are not results in frustration and despair. We also have a tendency to think that, compared with other notable figures, our circumstances are the least desirable and we are at the bottom of the heap, especially if we have not attained to society's benchmarks of success, namely - wealth, status or recognition.

Whereas celebrities were once imbued with an aura of

mystique, the dawn of the technological and information age has meant that the media now whets our appetite to know more and more about matters whose significance is less and less. How did we get to a point where we know more about a celebrity than our own grandmother; yet we must question whether what we know is really worth knowing. In an age of relentless information, we must establish boundaries on what we take in to guard against overwhelm and meltdown. Not to mention the fact, that our precious time is being squandered with trivialities.

World events of great significance have been knocked off the front pages to make room for scandal-mongering headlines. Consumers of news struggle to discern between relevant news and celebrity gossip and speculation. The media have succeeded in stimulating the public appetite for non-stop entertainment and a desire for fame.

We have been alienated from our true selves by focusing outside ourselves on the lives of others. But celebrities are not spared this neglect of self-hood. By having to focus on their fan base, the paparazzi and the media, they become overwhelmingly pre-occupied with how they are perceived. Many celebrities fear having their image undermined in any way. Their image is their brand; but they forget this, and it becomes fused with their identity.

Whatever station in life we may occupy, we all have endless opportunities to excel and influence others in a positive way, whether we are famous or not. It is the author's hope that this book will help to convince you that you are enough as you are, and that your life and dreams are worth celebrating and pursuing.

In my first book in the series *'Culture Detox Cleaning Our Minds from Toxic Thinking'*, I urged us to step aside from this cultural madness long enough to recognise it for the hollow and distorted reality that it is. I examined the roots of our cultural malaise and offered guidelines on de-junking our minds from the false values of our modern age. My thrust was the need to wake up from the state of our spiritual sedation which I identified as being dangerous for the following reasons:

- o We fail to see the popular culture for what it is – a hollow counterfeit having a 'placebo' effect.

- o Our spiritual senses become so dull that we lose our capacity to discern between good and bad. Because of our tendency to binge on the 'junk food diet' of what the culture has to offer, it leaves us spiritually malnourished and sick.[4]

We are victims of the way we see ourselves, not the way the world sees us. How many of us really love ourselves? In this modern world, we are encouraged to be so hard on ourselves. We berate ourselves for being overweight, then deny ourselves the necessary nourishment for our bodies. We become depressed when we make mistakes or life doesn't go according to plans. We criticise the way we look, we envy others and give up on our dreams, not because we really believe they are impossible but because we don't think we deserve to achieve them. After all, we tend to think, 'Who am I to think I can make a career out of …?' But why not? Others have done it, even against tremendous odds.

In this book - 'Culture Detox 2: Celebrating Self not Celebrity', I consider the ways in which we can realistically live in ways that are contrary to the values of the popular culture. I first look at the extent of the problem, then consider why we must change and how we can change.

Part 1: The Fantasy

Chapter 1: Entertainment

A fantasy may be defined as *"The faculty or activity of imagining impossible or improbable things"* or *"A fanciful mental image, typically one on which a person often dwells and which reflects their conscious or unconscious wishes."* [5] In a world with so many unpleasant realities, many of us choose to escape into a world of entertainment. That is what we tell ourselves, failing to realise that this pastime is not mindless and inconsequential, but on the contrary, it blocks and delays our *"conscious or unconscious wishes."*

Engaging in fantasy or what is commonly referred to as daydreaming, is a legitimate part of our human development. Nor is it limited to our childhood, but must form part of a healthy inner life for the whole of our lives. Rather than starring in our legitimate fantasies, we allow famous strangers to take our place and replace our dreams with futile imagination and speculation about them. We may think that entertainment by them is necessary because they do us a favour by helping to distract us from the unpleasant aspects of our lives, but the reality is that we all have unpleasant aspects of our lives, including them. It takes a compelling vision and huge effort to improve or eradicate these unpleasant aspects, no less so for them. It's easy to believe that celebrities, especially the ones we are drawn to, lead idealistic lives. Courtesy of the internet, we can get tours of their homes, guesstimates of their incomes, and peeks into their social circles. We envisage ourselves in their shoes because their lives seem so 'perfect' compared to ours.

In order to be entertained, we have come to believe that we have to switch on a device, or part with our hard-earned money to buy a product or attend an event, then sit back and be a passive spectator. We have lost the awareness that we can entertain ourselves, either by retreating into our imaginations, engaging in play such as 'playing a sport' or participating in social interactions where there is mutual sharing and enjoyment.

A popular pastime is for the family to gather around the television set as if it is the ultimate panacea for all ills. If the family is brought together around 'the small screen' to watch and discuss the highly anticipated episode of a popular TV show, awards show, or even the news, the focus becomes what's happening on the screen rather than the family. An opportunity is lost for family bonding and mutual enjoyment. What's worse, more often than not family members retreat to their own corner to fixate on their screen of choice, whether this be TV , laptop, Xbox, tablet, mobile phone and the list goes on.

The visual arts and industries fuel our imaginations and a need to escape from the 'rat race' of life. Some means of escape are more beneficial than others. For example, some quiz shows can help to stimulate the memory, and so stave off diseases such as Alzheimer's. Some documentaries can enlighten and provide information to help improve our understanding of life. Some YouTube videos actually furnish us with skills such as teaching, baking, DIY or how to be more financially adept. This book does not seek to decry all entertainment, but to focus specifically on the dangers of celebrity fixation.

It is also worth bearing in mind that just as we are not created to be entertained, in the original sense of the word, so too we were not created to be entertainers. Although we might be entertaining or entertain others from time to time, to see this as our sole purpose in life would be to limit ourselves to be constantly at the mercy of public approval. Also, no human being should be viewed as existing solely for the purpose of public observation and amusement. That would surely be a fate worse than being a caged bird and a blueprint for misery! Is it any wonder that so many of these so-called entertainers lead drug-laden and sad lives in reality – a far cry from the characters they portray and the wonderful lives the media often portray them as leading.

Although it has become the 'new normal' to disengage from life at the click of a button, is it really in the best interest of society as a whole. It is so seductive to believe that watching that box office film or our favourite star in their latest role will revive or refresh us, when it usually does the opposite. It is time-consuming, energy sapping and mind-numbing. Life itself is meant to be entertaining – replete with adventure, drama and discovery. We also have natural instincts to pursue adventures and explore new possibilities which, unlike entertainment, implies that we are active participants.

Our minds have also become casualties of the new approach to producing entertainment. Film and TV editors now cut scenes to short lengths so that the quick transition from scene to scene has effectively destroyed our concentration spans. Because entertainment is now so captivating with attention-grabbing special effects, we get easily bored with our own lives. Our everyday lives are filled with constant repetition of mundane tasks, and in real time our goals are achieved and dreams come to fruition far more slowly. We may daydream about what it would be like to live the life of a celebrity of choice, not realising that they too probably have their mundane tasks to attend to, and suffer their moments of boredom and frustration.

The need to always be in the spotlight and entertain an audience has been foisted on the lives of celebrities. A case in point is the Reality TV Series 'Keeping up with the Kardashians' where each episode shows a headline-grabbing development. It illustrates that what we require of celebrities is to be anything but boring. We resist factual portrayals of reality as it naturally unfolds. This 'slice of life' genre is no longer engaging in itself but must be 'spiced up' to hold the attention of the viewers. For example, David Attenborough's documentaries are edited with background music to heighten the sense of drama in nature.

News is now rarely presented by newscasters in grey suits. There are often dressed as if they are going to a social event, and the tendency to feature a solo presenter has given way to a duo or panel who discuss more light-hearted topics with banter and sometimes overly dramatic intensity. The public now gravitate towards the breakfast or daytime talk shows where sets are designed as if they are being invited into the hosts' living room for a casual chat. Commentary on the news is now more engaging than the news itself because the news is a non-stop cacophony of repeated events only distinguished by changes in names, faces and locations.

Chapter 2: Ultimate Achievement

Fame used to be considered a by-product of doing something well; now it is viewed as a worthy goal in itself. By contrast, to be invisible or unnoticed your whole life is considered by many wannabes to be a fate worse than death. The truth eludes us that it is better to matter deeply to one person in your life than be 'worshipped' from a distance by countless strangers. This may be part of the reason why many countries are experiencing an epidemic of loneliness; rather than cultivating meaningful relationships, our focus is on increasing our 'likes' and 'hits' on social media.

Achieving celebrity status is seen as the ultimate achievement. Not only have the number of celebrities proliferated because there are now celebrities in seemingly every industry, the amount of information has skyrocketed because of the internet. Most celebrities have a 'virtual' platform of preference where they promote themselves and their brand whether it be platforms such as Instagram, Snapchat, YouTube or personal web sites..

Have we not all dreamed of fame at one time or another? Fame is seen as a legitimate drug which the multitudes crave. What drives so many to achieve fame? Blogger, Kathy Benjamin, offers food for thought - *"There is usually some unacknowledged need that we think being famous will fix. If you don't feel like you get enough love or recognition from your parents or significant other, you might want millions of strangers to fill that gap."*[6]

The Case of Anna Nicole Smith (1967-2007)

> *An American model and actress, she was desperate to escape her past of poverty and nonentity status. She despised her upbringing so much she wanted to create and live in an alternate reality*[7] *Modelling herself on her own idol, Marilyn Monroe, she sought*

to transcend herself through plastic surgery and the creation of a larger than life alter ego, as well as marrying into billions. She became dependent on prescription medicines for various medical conditions which led to her tragic death from an accidental drug overdose at the age of 39.

We often think it's okay to desire fame but remain oblivious to the high price we will have to pay to acquire and maintain it. This is so often perceived as the route to escape from being a 'nobody'. You might think sub-consciously – 'The more people know me, the more important I am and the more my existence is validated.' You might become famous by accident, but holding on to it, is never by accident. This is comedically illustrated in the film 'Hero'/'Accidental Hero' (1992) where Bernie, an anonymous stranger becomes a hero overnight having rescued passengers from a burning plane. He happens to share his act of bravery with a friend who then poses as the hero to gain the reward money offered by the TV station. This impostor later regrets his duplicity because the public and media simply cannot get enough of him. Indeed, fame can be exhausting!

The focus of fame for many is not so much about contributing something of quality to mankind but making money. After all, the more products you have to sell, potentially the more money you stand to make. Also, the more products you make, the more people will need to be employed to make them. Thus fame becomes the capitalist dream which helps to turn the wheels of a capitalist economy. Yet, studies show that after we attain a certain level of economic well-being where our basic needs for food, shelter, clothing are being met, we do not become happier when we exceed this level. So, having or making a lot of money, does not satisfy the human craving for peace and contentment.

Perhaps we crave fame so much because we don't know

who we are or how much we are worth without it.

The Case of Jennifer Lopez

> *Singer, actor and dancer - Jennifer Lopez – declared in an interview with 'Red' Magazine – "fame does not give you self worth" [March 2019 issue]. In her book 'True Love' she confesses how she began to accept as truth the negative comments in the media and she temporarily lost herself in trying to live up to other peoples' expectations of her [p.23 'Rock Bottom'].*

There is always a danger of seeking validation outside yourself. The relationship between fans and the object of their adoration will always involve distance. The closer we get to people, the more we see their flaws up close and personal. The mystique is thereby removed and they lose their appeal.

Yet one of the modern criteria by which we measure success is now fame. It may cover a spectrum of degrees, from how many 'friends' you have on Facebook, 'connections' on Linked-In or Instagram 'likes', to whether you're considered a celebrity A-lister in Hollywood, Bollywood or Nollywood. Well-known indicators of fame consist of appearing on the covers of established magazines such as 'Time', 'People' or 'Forbes', whether you appear in wax at Madame Tussauds, or have a star on the Hollywood Walk of Fame.

Other indicators would be whether you're the winner of notable industry awards such as a 'Grammy', 'Oscar', 'Tony' or the like, are pursued by the paparazzi or whether people across the globe know you by your first name alone. This is the case with Oprah, or an amalgamation such as JLo, J-law or Kimye – a hybrid of Kim Kardashian and Kanye West, or Brangelina which was a mix of Brad Pitt and Angelina Jolie.

The adoring public seems largely unconcerned with how celebrities achieve their fame – the important factor is the fact that they're famous. There are some celebrities who are famous for being famous, but do not appear to have achieved anything of substance. They are dismissively known as 'famesque' – a term coined by Washington Post writer, Amy Argetsinger, and once used to describe Sienna Miller because of her association with Jude Law. This reductionist label seems unjustified as Miller formally studied the craft of acting at prestigious schools, is an American actress in her own right and has co-designed a fashion label with her sister, a fashion designer. Some achieve celebrity by being associated with or just by being related to someone who is famous. Fame can also be acquired posthumously as was the case with the American singer singer, Eva Cassidy and the Dutch painter, Vincent Van Gogh.

The media colludes with the famous by courting them and shining their spotlight on them because they have something to sell which countless thousands or millions want to buy. The public's appetite for what they have to sell is often manufactured using clever advertising strategies and gimmicks. For example the winsome smile of Julia Roberts has been used to sell perfumes because what woman would not want to be as 'happy' as she appears to be? She has been able to translate her appeal on the big screen to help advertise products. All advertising is based on the premise of convincing people they need to have something that in most cases they don't actually need.

Whether it's a block-buster film, a new music album, a beauty or fashion accessory or just sex appeal, this dance between the famous and the adoring fans, often reaches fever-pitch. Why? Because the media has stoked our imaginations by spinning convincing illusions. It would be nice to think there are a class of famous 'superhumans' who have mastered the secrets of life. The reality is that the vast majority of celebrities, though they have mastered a skill or craft we may admire, would not be worthy life mentors, nor do they desire to be.

Fame has been described as an addiction unlike any other. It pulls you into its tentacles and sucks the lifeblood of ordinariness out of you; suddenly being ordinary is no longer good enough – you crave recognition and kudos and feel this validates you more than the voice of your own soul and conscience. You risk becoming attached to a lifestyle that requires you be seen with the right crowd at the right holiday spots and your behaviour may have to become all the more outlandish and outrageous to spin headlines. Many child stars who acquire fame before their sense of self and value system are solidified, fall prey to its pressures.

The Case of River Phoenix (1970-1993)

He was dubbed a 'teen idol' who succumbed to a drug overdose at the age of 23, and is quoted as saying, "I wish I could go somewhere where nobody knows me."[8]

The downsides of fame identified by talent agents and managers in relation to their clients are "loss of privacy, being subjected to hyper criticism, fear and anxiety that the success can go away anytime, dealing with lies in the media, being taken advantage of by family and friends, being taken advantage of by professionals they employ, targeted by criminals, saying goodbye to *'everyday', normal life, stalkers, anxiety over feeling like an impostor."[9]* To be knocked off fame's pedestal would be a painful process of leaving the bright lights and once more slipping into darkness and obscurity. They would be pilloried in the press for losing this most precious of acquisitions. Most of the public, who secretly desire fame, would struggle to understand how those who choose simply to walk away from fame, could be so cavalier with something so enviable and elusive. Is it any wonder that many celebrities look so ill at ease with their status; so many are conflicted over the very thing which has brought them so much worldly recognition. On the one hand, it's an ego trip with many material gains; on the other hand, it also brings many losses.

The famous must walk a fine line between courting fame (often the gateway to their bread and butter) and pushing it away as an unwelcome intruder. Some relish their fame so much that they are able to disregard and overlook the obvious downsides such as intrusion into privacy. It is undeniable that there are certain celebrities who love fame. This might depend on personality types as well as age. Having an outgoing personality and finding fame at an older age, do appear to help as we see in the case of Will Smith, Henry Cavill and Woody Allen who describe being famous as more positive than not.[10]

The media now prefers to hone in on celebrity scandals; it seems that no aspect of the celebrity's life is off limits. Celebrities often feel they could be photographed or recorded on video at any time whether by the media, a stranger or a friend who might then leverage this for their own interests. It was abhorrent to think that in her dying moments following the car crash in the Paris tunnel on that fateful day - 31 August 1997, Princess Diana, was still being photographed. Everyone, no matter how famous, deserves a private life. After all, what could be more private than your dying moments? What she needed most was medical intervention and compassionate respect, not yet another photograph.

The Case of Princess Diana (1961-1997)

She was the picture of beauty, grace and charm, the

epitome of caring and giving – a true fairy tale
princess. She was described by the Daily Telegraph's
Royal Photographer, Ian Jones, as "the most
photographed woman in the world". Such was the
media frenzy around Princess Diana, that she
ushered in an age where no aspect of celebrities'
lives are off-limits.

Those who hunger and thirst for fame, not just the attainment but the sustaining of it, are compensating for some childhood deficiency. In most cases, it does not require a lot of digging to find the evidence of this. Celebrities are usually very prone to over-sharing as they are forever being interviewed. Confession is often good for the celebrity soul and it allows them to connect more deeply with their fan-base. This makes them more relatable; it's a type of inverse psychology to which the public are susceptible. In making them feel that celebrities are like them, prone to weakness and tragedy, they too are more likely to believe they too can one day achieve celebrity status. Furthermore, celebrity confessions spin more headlines and intrigue. It's as if the further a celebrity falls from the images of perfection we impose on them, the more they are having to 'atone' for their celebrity. After all, why should they have all the perks and none of the detriments, we think sub-consciously.

Many subscribe to the misconception that only famous people have done something remarkable with their lives, and that is why they're famous. The reality is that countless more people do remarkable things but will never become famous. Celebrity opinions are often sought on the talking points of the day as if they have been endowed with extraordinary wisdom and insight on virtually every topic, by virtue of their fame. It may be that the media houses are keen to snag a sound-bite or provocative comment which will attract more hits, viewers or listeners to their channel or publication. Because the media encourages to fixate on a select few celebrities at any given time – those who steal the headlines due to some newsworthy development in their lives or careers, we are never encourages to consider that there are countless others whose accomplishments are worth knowing about in the world.

TV has exposed us to the lives of the rich and famous in splendid detail, thereby whetting our appetites for more. We see these people so often – often much more than our family, friends and neighbours - that we think we know them. Celebrities encourage this faux connection because they are all too well aware that without their fan-base, they stand to lose money, work and possible a sense of self-worth. A subtle form of co-dependency can develop between fans and the famous whereby fans join communities for breaking news, special ticket prices and discounts on celebrity brands such as 'the beehive' of Beyoncé fans and Mariah Carey's 'lambily'. They are quick to savage any critics and come to their idol's defence, as well as extol all their virtues, despite having no personal relationship with them in real time. They risk becoming addicted to the dopamine rush for every update on any of their social media platforms whenever it arrives in their email inboxes. The benefits may appear to be mutual but, on closer examination, they tend to favour the celebrities whose profit margins and egos continue to expand at their fans' expense. Fans are thereby encouraged to devote more of their time and money to be part of their celebrity following.

Chapter 3: Fairy Tale Fixation

C elebrities are hyped up to such an extent that even they struggle to live up to the image in which they are cast. Who can be beautiful, well-dressed, articulate, funny or ooze talent at every waking moment of their lives? This public expectation often hounds them for the rest of their lives. We forget that behind the fairy tale image is an entourage of stylists, publicists, person trainers, cooks and the like all working in unison towards the common goal of ensuring that a celebrity is as marketable as possible.

The narrative tends to run like this: meet spouse of your dreams, get married, have a fairy tale wedding, followed by children to form a picture-perfect family. This means you now have what most people strive for and attain - a family, but with all the glitz and glamour surrounding this, it seems like perfection itself. Articles in the press will be crafted from the angle that this person has it all. This is designed to instigate envy in the readers which is also accompanied by a certain degree of daydreaming as they are transported into someone else's world for a brief moment.

The Case of Grace Kelly (1929 - 1982)

The wedding of Hollywood 'princess', Grace Kelly, to Prince Rainier III in 1956 captured the imaginations of onlookers from across the world. Little could they have ever imagined that on 14 September, 1982, she would sustain fatal injuries in a tragic car accident. Facts later came to light that her life was not the idyllic fairy tale it had been portrayed to be, and that she struggled to adjust to life as a princess in Monaco.

Modern fame obliges its stars to be conformed to an idealised image which is humanly impossible. From this perspective fame is dehumanising since at the core of being human is to be imperfect. This creates a no-win situation for those who become famous for their image. All human beings know and experience physical ageing and deterioration. Therefore, to be fêted and adored for one's image or looks alone is to be consigned to a shelf life where there is an expiry date on one's value to others. Female celebrity models who appear in front of the camera, are especially susceptible to this message, and often struggle with issues related to body image such as anorexia and bulimia. The timeline of how celebrities age, has become a common feature on YouTube. Certain channels shine a spotlight on physical features alone, and give celebrities the unrealistic impression that remaining 'young' and 'beautiful' is a 'duty'! ('Keep young and beautiful' lyrics written by Al Dubin for the film 'Roman Scandals', 1933).

Whenever self-perception is at the mercy of other peoples' perceptions, there will be an industry that will reap the benefits. That industry is the cosmetic surgery industry. Many women believe that this is the only way they can retain their good looks, and therefore safeguard their careers.

It has now become the norm for women in Hollywood or in the spotlight, and with the means to do so, to opt for plastic surgery. To be forever young is the fantasy which translates into being forever adored and desired. We overlook the fact that, not only is it unrealistic to remain young indefinitely, it would also mean that one's potential can never be realised.

Ironically, most people report greater life satisfaction once they are beyond the heady days of youth.[11] It is easy to be captivated by actors in particular roles when they exuded maximum charisma, strength, beauty or glamour. Because these performances on film can be replayed over and over again, these idealistic appearances become fixed in our minds, and it's easy to forget that they are ageing like the rest of us.

The reality is that the more often we see an image the more it sears itself into our sub-conscious as normative. In other words, it becomes an ideal of what should be rather than what is. Many impressionable people think that this is the acceptable way to look, rather than accepting that their looks are unique, and to be celebrated for that very reason. Body shaming is on the rise. We tend to judge solely by people's appearance so we are so easily shocked when the truth, like an air bubble, finally ripples to the surface. When will we learn that pictures lie? Hence, we should not be so shocked or traumatised when we see a celebrity without makeup or in a less flattering light.

Deep down we would like to think that someone has cracked it - the secret to eternal youth, never having a bad hair day, the perfect marriage and family. We are only setting them up for a fall and ourselves for disappointment. What's more, why would we think that these external ideals imply an absence of pain and suffering?

But there are other subplots and stereotypical characters in these fairy tales. The media, it would appear, decide on how they will portray you, and stick to it regardless. Human beings, with all their complex dualities, are portrayed as uni-dimensional caricatures.

From the power couple has been spawned a multi-headed monster called the celebrity family. The Will and Jada Smith and the Beckham clans are cases in point where each member is or is forecast to be a celebrity in his or her own right. This means that our attention is now divided to a greater degree. But it cuts both ways. In a subtle way, these celebrity parents are handing over the baton of fame to their offspring at an early age, preparing them for life in the public eye, but also preparing the public to receive them seamlessly into the ranks of celebrity status. There is money to be made from being a celebrity, and the family name and this is a guaranteed way of ensuring the family 'gravy train' will continue. The downside of this strategy is that they risk creating in the public a sense of entitlement to be voyeurs into their private lives across many generations.

It's easy to forget that there are a rare brand of private individuals who would not choose fame on any terms. Indeed, the best type of fame is the one that's freely chosen rather than thrust upon you by virtue of your surname, or association with others.

The pivotal question is - why would we want to follow in the footsteps of those who, in many cases, do not enjoy marriages which last, who marry several times, develop addictions or die at relatively young ages? We have cast them in a surreal light – imagining sub-consciously that their wealth, fame and glamour will make everything come out roses in the end. So when we hear chilling headlines of untimely death such as occurred with Michael Jackson, Elvis Presley and Whitney Houston, we are genuinely shocked and grieve, not so much the passing of the person we did not truly know but only knew about, but the fantasy of how we imagined them to be.

A way to reinforce the celebrity pre-occupation is to pair up celebrities so that their appeal is multiplied. When celebrities become couples or find a significant other, we somehow feel invested in their relationships as if we have a right to know. There is now no aspect of celebrity life that the media do not feel the need to pry into, for example there is a sense that they feel entitled to know when the couple are getting married, whether they will have children, how many and the preferred genders. In the wake of fake news and an over-reliance on photographs and untrustworthy journalism, it is now reasonable to question if a relationship is legitimate or just a marketing ploy. We can never know for sure what is true and what is not.

The guaranteed way to create a media sensation is to alight on a celebrity pairing. This can work with platonic friendship where there may be slight innuendo of something more, or it can be a full-blown, self-declared celebrity romance. There has been endless speculation about the platonic friendship between Leonardo Di Caprio and Kate Winslet[12]. There was a time when the idea that it could be anything more, would never have been entertained, simply because she is already married. The fact that they have played the roles of spouses or lovers on-screen, has only served to fuel this speculation. It is difficult for the public to know where fiction ends and reality begins.

The Western zeitgeist encourages the romantic notion of two soul-mates made for each other, and destined to be together. When these two soul-mates happen to be famous, the pairing takes on a particularly surreal and entrancing appeal. Very often these relationships do not last long-term, and then we become enticed by all the drama of the break-up. There tend to be two camps of followers which emerge – those who accept the break up and forget about it, and those who continue to hold on to the romantic delusion that they will get back together. There seemed to be a cultural wave of grief at the break up of Jennifer Aniston and Brad Pitt. This was triggered by the tidal wave of articles in the press on this subject especially discussions as to why they may have broken up as if we the general public have a right to know. When Jennifer Aniston finally found love again with Justin Theroux and re-married, their divorce which ensued three years later, seemed to re-ignite the rumour mill that she and Brad had re-united. The question arises why do we invest so much interest in other peoples' personal relationships, especially those whom we do not know?

Celebrity pairing has become a huge guessing game and a relentless activity for the press. Very often people sighted together are suddenly presumed to be going out. From week to week, it is often unclear for some who they are going out with. The press speculation and often deliberate misrepresentation has created a lot of misinformation, and often celebrities feel duty bound to clarify these misrepresentations by the press by issuing a public statement. It should never have been necessary for Jennifer and Justin to issue a rebuttal following their separation. It read as follows – *"In an effort to reduce any further speculation, we have decided to announce our separation... We are two best friends who have decided to part ways as a couple, but look forward to continuing our cherished friendship. Normally, we would do this privately, but given that the gossip industry cannot resist an opportunity to speculate and invent, we want to convey the truth directly."*[13] However, we can never hope to know the full truth about other peoples' personal relationships, nor should we have such unrealistic expectations.

For a celebrity to be alone seems a grave injustice to the fans because we want their lives to be a fairy tale – scripted like a hallmark romance. It's as if we forget that they are only human after all. For actors and performers in general, we forget that they only play fictional roles but that most of their lives are lived off camera where they too must wrestle with demons, overcome heartache and heartbreak and deal with all the challenges of being a human being. It's as if we prefer to buy in to the mass delusion fuelled by the media that they are super-humans who are automatically destined to marital bliss and longevity by virtue of their celebrity. No sooner are we adjusting to the news of a break up, then a groundswell of speculation mounts as to who the newly single celebrity might be dating. There are lists on the internet ranging from celebrities who are dating, who are married, who have been married the longest, whom we don't know were married, who had secret weddings, and whose relationships are conjectured not to last. The list goes on and on. It's easy to find yourself swept along on a tide of endless guessing which, when all is said and done, bears no relevance to your real life.

Perhaps the serial monogamy which seems to be spun as the norm in Hollywood is due to the fact that the celebrities believe that they are playing roles rather than truly being themselves. Could it be possible that they too have forgotten themselves? After all, if the real you does not show up to the relationship, how can there be any hope of success? It just may be possible that those who are drawn to the entertainment industry are those who disliked being themselves so much that they sought a livelihood from playing other people. The hardest role that any of us will ever play is ourselves.

The Case of Zsa Zsa Gábor (1917-2016)

She was an American film &TV actress who is best remembered for her nine marriages, seven divorces and one annulment. Because she was romantically linked with some of the biggest Hollywood stars of the day, she was dubbed "the most successful courtesan of the 20th century". Gábor is recognised as having ushered in a new age of celebrity following based on her personal life rather than her career.

Sir David Beckham went on record during an interview as stating that *"marriage is hard work and not a fairy tale"*.[14] But surely this is a statement of the patently obvious; although most prefer to believe the myth that for a select few it comes easily. The reality is that sadly most celebrity marriages end up on the rocks. Good looks and star quality alone, do not successful relationships make. In so doing, he may have been voicing a subliminal wish to be regarded as a normal human being, and not a superhuman. After being fêted for over two decades by the press, it would be practically impossible for him to be ever perceived again as 'ordinary'.

The unspoken truth is the fact that relationships require space and privacy in order to thrive. Any detailed knowledge of a personal relationship should be by invitation and not imposition, and by trusted friends and confidants. If a relationship is influenced by public pressures or press speculation, like a fragile flower, it is in danger of breaking.

The myth of the fairy tale is heightened by Red Carpet events. The symbiosis of the entertainment and fashion industries is perfectly illustrated by the 'Met Ball' – an annual, fundraising gala hosted by the Metropolitan Museum of Art's Costume Institute, New York. Each year there is a theme and many celebrities appear on the red carpet with their inspired ensembles based on this theme. Through such Red Carpet events, and fashion runways during fashion weeks in various cities of the world at various times of the year, the fashion industry has become more entertaining and entertainment is now more fashion-conscious.

Many celebrities now see it as a cachet to be snapped by the paparazzi, and so make an effort not to leave the house without looking their best or most flamboyant. It's a type of free advertising, and who knows, they might get a cosmetic or clothing brand deal as a result of all the media attention.

We are all now privy to the photo albums of those in the limelight. They post their wedding, birthday party, even children's births on Instagram or make them available to magazines. What used to be a private affair, is now in the public domain. It may feel as if you are privy to the photo album of a close friend, but the reality could not be further from the truth. It makes more sense to spend time looking at our own photo albums which have the potential to trigger powerful memories. In a graphically charged society, we are accosted by a virtual avalanche of photos. It becomes increasingly difficult to discern which are important and relevant and which should be quickly dismissed or disregarded. Ordinary folk have become inspired by these 'celebrity weddings' to spend obscene amounts of money on their own weddings even thought they can barely afford it.

We form and express opinions about celebrities as if we know them. Also, the public's ability to comment online on any news story has meant that opinion now trumps truth. We have lost sight of the fact that the press only gives us tidbits of information about them – most of which would be deemed inadmissible in a court of law, and yet we are so quick to pass judgement.

Words and pictures don't always match or align with accuracy. This then leaves readers confused as to what to believe.

Why are we so inquisitive about the private lives of celebrities? They are really no different from us. Like us, they desire love and stability. We have cast them in the involuntary roles of Reality TV stars in which their highs, lows and intimate moments inform the scripts. The media goes so far as to put words in their mouths as if they are reading from pre-determined scripts.

We have been conditioned to unceasingly compare people especially in terms of how they look or what they have accomplished. It's a talking point for the media, but we may be oblivious to the fact that they have spun a false narrative just to exploit the fame of celebrities for profit.

What we see of celebrities often contradicts the story we

later hear about their suffering, trauma and habit of putting on a brave face. More and more opportunities are being engineered to give us a glimpse of the celebrity lifestyle. For example, after-show parties at events such as 'The Oscars' are now featured in the media. It's not enough to see the pre-show walk on the Red Carpet, we have now been given a glimpse into what happens afterwards. These are split second photos but if you put them together, they create a 'show-reel' of what we think happened rather than what actually happened. We assume from the high octave smiles, and sparkling dresses that they had a great time. These supposedly private moments (after all these parties are not open to the general public), have become public but only to give us teasers of all the fun that was had, and which we missed. This only serves to whet our appetites for more celebrity news.

Part 2: The Flaws

Chapter 4: Behind the Public Image

An image is how someone appears to the public. This may be at odds with how they really are. As members of the public, we can become very invested in the images of the celebrities we favour. We are often reluctant for that image to change. We forget that they are human beings who of necessity must evolve and grow, and make mistakes.

The relentless pursuit of fame usually results from a deep-seated sense of dissatisfaction with the circumstances of their lives before they were famous, whether in the form of poverty, abandonment, bullying, abuse, rejection or low self-esteem. On the surface, fame appears to be the best answer to all these horrors; the young child often imagines, 'when I am famous, I will never be poor, abandoned, bullied, abused rejected or suffer low self-esteem again'. The reality is often so different for those who attain celebrity. It soon becomes clear that all these inner and outer realities may still plague them. For example, fame would never be enough for Michael Jackson. His underlying, driving urge, at every stage of his life, seemed to be to re-kindle the childhood he had lost.

Celebrity is for many a search for the love which they never received as children. For those who received such love, they have grown up to be sufficiently self-assured that they do not crave the love and attention of thousands, if not millions, of adoring fans. Granted, fame does not necessarily stem from hubris or ego. The Greek word for self-love, 'philautia', infers self-esteem which is different from self-confidence. The downward spirals of many celebrities into addiction to drugs, alcohol and other dangerous substances and activities, suggests a lack of 'philautia' which is the foundation of psychological well-being.[15] Branding of celebrities puts people in pigeon holes. For example, Oprah has become known as the 'moral compass of our times' and a spiritual thought leader in her own right. On 'the Oprah Winfrey show' she interviewed people from all walks of life for 25 years, followed by the founding of her spirituality-seeking OWN Network where she delves even more deeply into the discussion of spirituality and purposeful living. Many followers expect that all her views on all aspects of life will be correct. The same may hold true for other national icons who exude wisdom and insight such as Dr Oz and Dr. Phil. This means that we conveniently don't need to think for ourselves; rather we can be content to follow and quote such luminaries. In this way, they become idols even though this may be neither their intent nor ours.

No one would blame celebrities for having to be more self-conscious about their appearance, than the average person. Could this explain their predilection for what many would deem unnecessary plastic surgery. After all, look at yourself enough times, and you're bound to see some flaws. The tabloids have taken celebrity scrutiny to the extreme of commenting on body parts not just general appearance. To be saddled with the scrutiny of each body part is often reserved for women who are particularly set up for such ageism.

The Case of Jennifer Aniston

> *Though known as an actor, various parts of her body have been heavily scrutinised and commented on for the better part of her career. From movie roles where her physical features are emphasised, to her double crown of 'People's Most Beautiful Woman'; from the 'Rachel' hair, to whether or not she is pregnant, her physicality seems to be her stock in trade. Though her interviews convey a thespian eager to fine tune her craft and be taken seriously, this is overshadowed by the more superficial aspects of her life.*

Media perceptions of a celebrity are repeated so often that

they become assimilated into public consciousness as reality. On closer inspection, their lives are just as complex and problematic as the next person's. They too may have hang-ups, fears and anxieties although they sport self-assured smiles, and luxurious outfits. Just like the rest of us, they have their weaknesses and insecurities.

There was a time when we wanted our celebrities in bubbles. It was as if we had placed them in 'glass houses' at which few if any stones were thrown. The public colluded with the media in preserving the edifice of myths surrounding their lives. We liked casting them in 'perfect' roles so we could escape into the myth of how wonderful their lives were, compared to how humdrum ours were. To illustrate a popular myth which has endured for decades, in the aftermath of President JFK's assassination on November 22nd, 1963, his widow Jacqueline Kennedy spun the Camelot legend as a worthy comparison for his political legacy and family life during his time in the white House. It has been very difficult to remove this myth from public consciousness even to this day.[16]

In recent times, the trend in journalism is to seek ways to infiltrate and burst that bubble, thereby unmasking the skeletons and less than complimentary aspects of celebrities' lives. As a result, negative news has skyrocketed. The view among the media pundits and players seems to be that bad news sells whether it's full blown scandal, tragedy or just a frisson of mischief or innuendo. But if we are conditioned to expect the worse in others, then how can we learn to expect the best for ourselves?

On the flip side, we may be blinded by celebrity worship to ugly and inconvenient truths. If the stars we adore, are guilty of egregious flaws or crimes, do we dismiss it as incredible or a sleaze campaign despite the overwhelming evidence? We seem to want celebrities to be perfect, or to have the ability to rebound perfectly and seamlessly from tragedy just like the heroes and heroines in fantasy fiction, so that we too can hope for a better version of our current selves and lives. Only those who are wise and perceptive or who step over into the other side of celebrity, know the truth – that their lives are just as challenging, open to vicissitudes and full of ugly skeletons, most often best left buried, just as ours are. Unless celebrities actually break the law, should we give any more attention to their bad behaviour than we would to our own.

Similarly, it is becoming the trend for celebrities to share their private moments, and thoughts including medical diagnoses, with the public through largely confessional auto-biographies and talk show interviews. There was a time when celebrities wanted to be adored from a distance, but now they want desperately for the fans to relate to them. Every celebrity lives with the inner awareness that they have certain struggles or have experienced certain traumas. They may harbour the fear that they will be exposed by the media, and so they preempt this 'public shaming' by taking to the celebrity 'media couch' to voluntarily confess all. It may genuinely be a form of therapeutic purging, or a way to grab headlines, sell books and become even more famous.

Whenever something tragic happens to a celebrity, we are reminded that they are only human after all.

The Case of Karen Carpenter (1950-1983)

Originally the drummer then the lead singer in 'the Carpenters', she became overly concerned about how she was perceived in terms of her physical appearance. This was reportedly triggered by a reporter's comment which led to her becoming convinced she needed to lose some weight, and this lead to a compulsive need to be thin and body dysmorphia. She fell captive to anorexia nervosa which is characterised by excessive purging to remain thin. Finally her heart gave way at the age of 32.

It could be that the celebrity you are hero-worshipping because of an image of them which has been captured and publicised in a magazine, is at this very moment lying sick in bed, depressed, suicidal or even dead. This would have happened with the likes of Marilyn Monroe and Anna Nicole Smith, and even more recently with Whitney Houston. It wasn't until they died, that we realised how miserable they had been. It is mind-boggling that these three women who captivated the whole world, could have been captive to so much addiction and emotional turmoil.

Also, disturbing truths can come to light in the aftermath of a celebrity's death – truths which they may have tried very hard to conceal whilst they were alive. Michael Jackson's later career was riddled with allegations of child sexual abuse. The 'not guilty' verdicts were somehow tarnished by the fact that he still gave compensation to one of the accusers. The 'Leaving Neverland' documentary has brought up fresh allegations from two men, now adults, who have recorded in harrowing detail, the nature of the abuse. One of the accusers, Wade Robson, stated, *"the abuse didn't feel strange because it was being done by this man that was like a god to me."*[17] The outcome of the civil suits which are being brought by these two men against Jackson's estate, is still pending at the time of publication. What remains undeniable is that the reputation of 'the King of Pop', who painted himself as a protector and advocate of children, has been forever tarnished.

Celebrities can be alleged victims as well as accusers. It was hard to swallow the unimaginable confession that the indomitable, feisty Mel B of 'Spice Girls' girl band fame, had contemplated suicide as a result of her harrowing experience of domestic abuse. Very often we only view our admired celebrities through uni-dimensional lenses. But in reality, human beings are a lot more complex with layers and dimensions. Also, their celebrity does not shield them from any of the challenges faced by others who are not famous.

The spate of celebrity confessional memoirs which are being published, shows that celebrities want us to be aware of their vulnerabilities – so that we will appreciate that they are only human after all. Similarly, the genre of documentary/exposé is now a regular feature at film festivals and at the box office. The controversy they tend to spark, prominent examples being 'Surviving R Kelly' and 'Amy', the Amy Winehouse documentary 2015, tend to show the less admirable side of celebrities. In the past, it was considered the norm only to show their virtues as if exceptional talent in one arena was equivalent to moral goodness.

Every now and then a celebrity experiences a crisis or tragedy which reminds us that they are just as human as we are – they suffer a bereavement, become captive to an addiction, experience a failed relationship or sudden, shocking incident or premature death. When Britney spears and Miley Cyrus went off the rails, this was played out in the media in a soap-opera like way, thereby blurring the lines between reality and fiction. When the average person has a meltdown, nobody cares, and it does not become the subject of public discussion and speculation.

Chapter 5: The Price of Fame

The privileges of being a celebrity mean that they get to live in their own worlds that are diametrically different from the way most people live. That is not to say their lives are devoid of problems. For the most part, they want us to believe they are just like us, and although we are all human, what they can afford, and the privileges they are granted put them in a certain stratosphere most can only dream of.

It may be argued that this bubble has a dual effect – it keeps people in and keeps other people out. Amongst celebrities, the late Michael Jackson is best known for his reclusive and eccentric lifestyle whenever he was not performing– marked by an ever-present entourage, face mask, his sprawling homes and expensive toys such as the Neverland Valley ranch he purchased. His 'bubble' was not fully deflated on his demise. Michael Jackson was showcased posthumously in a hologram and a DVD about the behind-the-scenes rehearsals for his London sell-out 'O2 Arena Tour'. He never lived to perform the first show. To illustrate further, there has been a non-stop cloning of Elvis Presley impersonators even though 'the King' has been dead since 1977. Similarly, Marilyn Monroe arguably has become more famous in the aftermath of her death than in her relatively short-lived 36 years.

The downside of the bubble is that for such celebrities the myth will become reality – they will begin to believe that the world revolves around them. With an entourage at their beck and call, and adoring fans waiting for autographs at the boundary of the bubble, it will be difficult not to start believing all the praise and hype. Human beings do not have the built-in mechanisms to deal with such idolisation, and so many celebrities turn to chemical substances to escape from the fanfare and the pressures of public expectation.

For some celebrities, the bubble becomes a cage which is an incursion on their freedom; for others it is desirable security to keep the deranged fans, stalkers and crazies at bay. Some welcome the bubble of celebrity because they would rather not have to rub shoulders with the masses. Whilst others want to blend in with the masses, others want to stand out from them. The latter tend to want to ensure that their fame lasts as long as possible because their former lives of anonymity paled by comparison, or may even have been downright demeaning in some way particularly if they suffered some manner of childhood trauma.

Celebrities often experience a profound sense of isolation because in the back of their minds will lurk doubts as to who they can trust. The rich and famous are always vulnerable to exploitation. What used to be considered private and confidential can be leaked into the public arena such as conversations or more intimate moments. It's difficult to remain psychologically sound when you have these fears forever lurking at the back of your mind.

People pursue fame for various reasons such as to boost a fragile self-esteem, find love and acceptance through adoring fans, secure a coveted income and lifestyle. If you pursue fame to be known and affirmed by as many people as possible as a goal in itself, you may not necessarily be investing in yourself/your life, and so your life can still fall apart. Yet, fame is often perceived by those who idolise fame itself as a ticket to an earthly paradise.

In modern times, it is widely exploited by those who have it, as a platform for selling products. The famous, at least the more business savvy among them, are keen to develop their own brand with which they hope to conquer the world and rake in millions. To be a celebrity and not make money from it, would be seen as a wasted opportunity by the majority who perceive it as the ultimate achievement. Most celebrities would espouse the ethos so poignantly captured by Oscar Wilde that *"The only thing in life worse than being talked about, and that is not being talked about."*

We have not yet realised that all this frenetic self-promotion is fuelled by the age-old human greed or the need to keep financially afloat and stave off the creditors. At the bottom of it all is usually the bottom line. A case in point is the 'King of Pop' whose comeback tour at the O2 arena in London, was cancelled by his premature death at the age of 50. The question arises - Why did he agree to do 50 shows in the light of his health challenges which were confirmed by the fact that he had a personal physician as part of his entourage whilst on tour. Conrad Murray was later convicted of involuntary manslaughter which caused the death of Jackson from an excessive administration of the anaesthetic propofol.

'The show must go on' mantra may sometimes belie the fact that a celebrity is at a crisis point and needs to take some time off. Demi Lovato was forced to do just this as she suffered a setback in her struggles with mental health and drug addiction. This led to a sudden cancellation of her Atlantic City concert in July 2018 so she could seek emergency treatment in hospital[18]. In an age of the 'celebrity confession' couch, her reputation will probably not suffer for cancelling her concerts at the last minute, although no doubt fans will be disappointed. How we wish Amy Winehouse had taken all the time she needed to make a proper recovery. The same can be said of Whitney Houston. These were songstresses who left this mortal clime far too young with so much more to offer, due to the ravages of their addictions.

Our sense of familiarity with celebrities is influenced largely by images. This is disturbing in itself because the information relayed by an image is often very superficial. The fact that so many people feel entitled to comment on the physicality of celebrities, is even more troubling. The high price of fame seems to be that you become fair game for people's opinions about how you look. Body shaming has become trendy amongst trolls.

Most celebrities do not set themselves up as being perfect, yet they are held up to impossible high standards. There was a time when comment was reserved for their work, for example theatre reviews or analysis of sporting competitions, but now all aspects of their lives invite comment and criticism. This says more about the critics than the celebrities. The popular culture now seems to endorse criticism ironically by celebrities themselves, known as 'celebrity judges', on shows such as 'America's Got Talent', 'British Bakeoff' and 'American Idol'. Shows such as 'Big Brother' invite the viewing public to vote on their preferred competitor.

What does it say about us if we regularly take part in this time-consuming and non-productive habit of criticising and making fun of celebrities who are most often in the news and therefore the subject of public discussion? It's easy to destroy a life but very challenging to build one. If you choose the former, it means that you have essentially checked out of the challenging business of building your own life, and have opted for an easy life that will bear little fruit. Our fixation on celebrities may be just a way of avoiding the challenges in our own lives.

The Case of Justin Bieber

He has shared his struggles with not being able to go outside without being hounded by photographers, and the isolation of being on tour when you're stuck in your hotel room because of the paparazzi and fans camping outside the hotel[19].

Fame often comes at a very high price. To not have the attribute of fame, is not the equivalent of being lack-lustre, but just plain human. Every human being needs privacy, needs space to grow and take risks and make mistakes without being criticised for every move they make. Fame puts you in a box from which it is so difficult to break free.

Chapter 6: Controlled by the Fan Base

A celebrity once stated, "I've been addicted to almost every substance known to man at one point or another, and the most addicting of them all is fame." This anonymous quote was derived from a study on fame in which 15 celebrities from various industries in the US, were interviewed to glean their perspectives on fame.[20]

A downside of celebrity that is often overlooked is that celebrities themselves only view their lives through the filter of their fame. They fail to consider who they were before they were famous, and who they will be after they are famous. They may forget the fact that at their core, they are human beings who have the same struggles, fears and concerns as everyone else. Ultimately, their celebrity is just an accoutrement or an 'outfit' which they wear but it is not the real them. They may struggle to forget that they are famous because they constantly see themselves the way others see them. Hence, their fame can become a trap, and they may find themselves longing to just 'be'. They may think they have to be 'switched on' and hyper-aware of their surroundings all the time just in case they get randomly photographed or assaulted by a lunatic fan. They may be fearful of saying how they really feel about a subject in case they are recorded and it's put on the internet. They will be prone to constantly second-guessing the motives of those they have in their inner circle, wondering if these people genuinely care about them or are simply after what they can get – whether money, favours, self-promotion or the simple prestige of being seen with someone who is famous which is how many pursue their own path to fame.

The Case of Joan Crawford (1904 - 1977)

Joan Crawford, the American actress who came to prominence in the early twentieth century, famously stated that "Alcoholism is an occupational hazard of being an actor, of being a widow, and of being alone. And I'm all three."[21] Even those with a talent for imagining and pretence, cannot simply wish away the real challenges of their existence. Joan Crawford was careful to cultivate a certain image which did not always sync with reality such as that of being the 'perfect mother'. In her autobiography 'Mommie Dearest', her daughter shared details of the childhood abuse she suffered at the hands of her adoptive mother.

Mariah Carey is always seen in full makeup and either wears heels or walks on tiptoe. She has also affected a certain way of speaking where sentences usually end with the affectionate drawl "Dahling". She is always smiling for the camera no doubt because she dreads a bad picture, but the reality is that no-one can be happy all the time, and she has recently been candid about her long struggle with bipolar disorder.

We demand that our stars always look their best, and we have convinced ourselves that they can morph magically into their on-screen personas portrayed in their heyday. Hence, we do not remember Elizabeth Taylor as she was in her final months of life, but in her stunning incarnation in 'Cat on a Hot Tin Roof' or we prefer to envisage Faye Dunaway, not as the 70+ year old she currently is, but as the 'femme fatale' she embodied in 'Thomas Crown Affair' or 'Bonnie & Clyde'. This illusion can be maintained by the press of a button on the DVD remote control.

When we read about a celebrity facing the challenges of a disease, divorce or bankruptcy, we gasp in amazement. Why? Because we have fallen for the myth that their lives are perfect, or at least far better than ours, simply because they are famous. We have entertained a false narrative that they can get anything they want, be with anyone they want, and have instant access to a social world that many of us can only dream of, and sometimes that they can even get away with anything.

The challenge of celebrities who have become a larger than life brand is that they will feel hard pressed to conform to the standards of what the fanbase deem acceptable and unacceptable behaviour or comments. For example, JLo stated her view that *"all lives matter"* as a counter to the *"Black Lives Matter"* mantra[22]. Instead of being praised as inclusive which is what the words mean on the face of it, she has been criticised for failing to understand the unique merits of the movement.

Similarly, Mariah Carey has been criticised for her meeting with sportsman, Colin Kapernick – former NFL player[23] who sparked controversy for his political gesture of kneeling during a pre-game playing of the national anthem, to protest police brutality against people of colour and racial injustice. The backlash caused by these publicised uploads suggests that fans were willing to withdraw their support for a celebrity because they do not necessarily espouse their views on social issues. This could lead to many celebrities bending their opinions and behaviour to suit a contingency of strident fans, simply out of fear of losing the revenue generated by their fan base. Perhaps performers in general are driven by a relentless desire to please which underpins their rise to stardom. We may think they are confident when in fact, their egos may be very fragile.

We have attributed to them qualities of being 'superhuman' for far too long. Now, we also admire qualities of survival and overcoming great obstacles against the odds. After all, everyone loves a comeback. The singer, Tina Turner, is as famous for having survived domestic abuse at the hands of her former husband and manager, as she is for her unique singing voice and energetic onstage performances.

Should we be separating the artists from their art form?

What about Whitney Houston who sang resonant, sublime gospel music but was a drug addict? Should we separate R Kelly from his music and boycott all his songs in the wake of his sexual abuse allegations? This may sound socially conscious in theory but in practice, where does this lead? Which failings will warrant such boycott and which are we willing to tolerate. This would mean that no artist's work could stand the test of scrutiny into their personal lives. We would all become guilty of throwing out the baby with the bath water. Ultimately, uncovering the ugly truth of celebrities' lives, whilst providing talking points for a brief period, only serve to highlight the age-old truth of human nature being capable of the worst and the best at the same time.

The famous must walk a fine line between courting fame (often the gateway to increased riches) and pushing it away as an unwelcome intruder. The downside to courting fame is that you are more likely to believe the hype, and your ego become inflated. If you think you are super-human, untouchable and can get away with anything because of your fame, are you then more likely to become another Harvey Weinstein or Bill Cosby? Their scandals and the malfeasance with which they have been accused by so many, illustrates the worst excesses of celebrity behaviour and abuse of power.

We often only see one side of celebrity – the public side of glamour and adulation. We no longer see the famous for the flawed human beings that they are, just as we are. They have become caricatures in a never-ending play in which they never really die because the story lines associated with them continue to run and run. Sadly, Bobbi Kristina Brown, the daughter of Whitney Houston, generated more media interest and headlines during the seven months she was in a coma and subsequently died, than she did when she was conscious and well.

Celebrities are being churned out at a frenetic pace such that fame has become fickle. Now everyone seeks '15 minutes of fame', but only a rarefied group get to hold on to it for longer. Usually, they have to re-invent themselves time and time again as the public easily tires of the same image, having become used to new images and headlines being spawned on a daily basis. Many celebrities have spawned lookalikes and impersonators. Although this may seem like a glamorous gig, it begs the question of when the 'wannabe' lookalikes get to be themselves. No human being was ever meant to be a carbon copy of another; even identical twins have unique traits as individuals.

Because so many celebrities generate an image which forms part of their brand, they feel duty bound or contractually obligated to constantly play the part, or keep their real selves well-hidden. In the posthumous Whitney Houston documentary – 'Can I Be Me?' it was clear that Whitney wanted to break free from all the constraining expectations of her brand or image. Perhaps this is why she turned to drugs as a way of escaping the relentless pressure. Sadly, her sweet escape soon turned into an ugly addiction to drugs which led to her undoing in the end.

The media are so hungry for news stories on so-called A-listers that certain publications will not flinch at putting out a dubious headline just to whet the public appetite for scandal, and booby-trap the celebrities into making a comment. After all, it takes a lot of self-restraint to resist denying an outright lie particularly when your reputation is at stake. The dilemma many celebrities face is that is they go down this road of denials, they may then become caught up in a never-ending swirl of rebuttals. This loss of control over how one is perceived can be emotionally crippling if one's ego is wrapped up in public approval. Justin Bieber and his wife Hilary Baldwin are in the habit of responding to their critics on social media[24]. Although it's instinctive to want to defend your name and reputation, it's a no-win situation for celebrities to engage in this war of words with those whose sole aim is to stoke the fires of controversy to generate media headlines.

For the most part it is perceived that a large degree of oversharing is required to keep the fans satisfied. Interviewers are prepped to ask the question that everyone wants to ask even if it is not pertinent to the primary focus of the interview. Usually it involves an intrusion into the private life of the celebrity. This also heightens their sense of being used just for commercial manipulation, and not being valued for their humanity. Having a solid base of family and friends who do value you as a person and not for your popularity or bankability is what will ensure emotional well-being in the midst of such a false reality.

Many celebrities are saddled with the lifelong burden from an early age of being the main breadwinner in the family. We may project unto them the motivation of performing for the sheer joy of expressing themselves artistically or leading a glitzy and glamorous lifestyle. The reality may be simply to put food on the table and pay the unceasing cascade of bills for goods and services needed to maintain their expensive lifestyles.

The Case of Judy Garland (1922-1969)

> *She was signed to MGM studios at the age of 13,*
> *and there she learned the need to be a workhorse*
> *as well as starve herself in order to remain slim.*
> *Thus began her lifelong struggle with eating*
> *disorders and body image.*[25]

There is a cycle to becoming a celebrity; the last stage is always mistrust. They begin to question why people want to be with them, and their personalities become split into two – the private self and the public self.[26] Beyoncé refers to her alter ago, Sasha Fierce, whom she morphs into when she's on stage. Mariah Carey refers to her alter ego as Bianca and she has featured in some of her music videos.

Part 3: The Fans

Chapter 7: The Cultural Language of

Idolatry

An idol is a 'graven image' or to put it in more modern terms, a cultivated image. Images have a way of searing themselves into our imaginations where they can dominate our lives.

An idol is anything other than God that demands your soul, mind and strength. An idol may also be defined in terms of the time you dedicate to thinking, talking or acquiring knowledge about this adored person. Although celebrity images are not moulded or carved by their fans who literally bow down to them, those who place them on a pedestal to be worshipped, do other acts which demonstrate their homage. They may sacrifice a lot of money to buy their merchandise. They may follow them on social media. They may speak about them as if they are gods with words such as 'I adore ...', 'I idolise ...', '... is the most beautiful, talented, amazing ... ', '... is GOAT' which translates as 'the Greatest Of All Time.' Fans will long to see this person in the flesh. This explains why fans go to celebrity signings, openings and concerts in the hope that they can catch a glimpse of this person, or if fortune smiles on them, get to have a selfie or a brief conversation or touch their skin in some way.

An addiction to a celebrity or celebrities may not seem like an addiction because it has become normalised. We can be easily swept along on a tide of popular opinion and social habits. The word 'groupie' has now been replaced by fan, and various umbrella terms are now used to describe fans of particular celebrities. So, for example, Mariah Carey fans are members of the 'lambily'; Beyoncé fans belong to the 'Beehive' and Demi Lovato fans are referred to as Lovatics. This was happening as far back as the sixties when the Beatles were all the rage, and their fans became referred to as 'Beatlemaniacs'. Once a member of the adoring public proclaims membership in one of these groups, it's akin to being the member of a football team. Your loyalty is expected and assured, and you will rise to defend the goodness and infallibility of your favourite artist with all the defiance of a well-trained bulldog.

We have an intrinsic need to worship; God made us this way. It has become perverted and is instead channelled towards counterfeit gods or idols of our own making. Let's face it – we make and break our celebrities; our imaginations mould them into what we want them to be, and when they no longer serve their purpose, we replace them with different ones. This cycle can continue for our entire lives or until we find our way back to the real God. He sought to protect us from this dangerous cycle of fake worship by instructing us *"Do not make idols of any kind ..."* (Exodus 20:4 NLT) These idols will steal our time, energy and ability to focus on the things which really matter. We will lose all motivation to worship the true God, and may not even recognise His existence. We are further told that *"... those who come to God must believe that He is, and that He rewards those who diligently seek him."* (Hebrews 11:6)

There was a time when idols were limited to physical objects which were fashioned into a desired image. Idols have been broadened to include human beings who can only be in one place at a time but whose images are replicated and preserved through digital photography and videos and film technology. Even when they are dead, these images continue to be circulated giving us the impression they are still alive.

By worshipping other human beings like ourselves, is this not another manifestation of self-love? In TV talent competitions such as 'American Idol', the contestants are often asked who they aspire to be like when they appear on stage. Our idols are usually more glamorous, talented, idealised versions of ourselves. But our idols also have their own idols, so they are conscious of the fact that they are not the ultimate, and also striving to be like someone else they too admire.

By contrast, the very essence of the true, living God is that He is perfect and complete, lacking nothing. He has no need to improve on Himself, and nothing can detract from His perfection. False gods or idols blind us to the true, living God who alone is worthy of worship. Just as how we often do not show up in our own lives because we are so distracted, they often do not show up for us. Concert and tour cancellations are commonplace, as occurs when a celebrity is sick, undergoing rehab, or dead. Even when they show up, their performances may be less than stellar, confirming that they are human after all. LL Cool J entitled his 2000 album G.O.A.T - 'the Greatest Of All Time'. It was a clever marketing ploy, and the expression became adopted by popular culture in general.

Celebrity culture has burgeoned to almost breaking point, threatening to hijack our minds to absorption with the trivial and the pointless. If the adoring public is so inclined, they can be apprised of the daily photographic postures and poses of their chosen celebrity, and their soundbite tweets. With the emergence of the internet and its various apps such as YouTube, Instagram, Snapchat and Twitter – and all other various forms of social media – it's all too easy for other peoples' lives to seem more compelling than our own. There is a subtle difference between admiring and adoring, but it makes all the difference on the impact these choices have on our lives. We have the power, mainly purchasing power, but at a more fundamental level through the choice to pay attention to them or not, to divest them of their celebrity status in our eyes regardless of how they are viewed in the media or by the masses. Most fans don't realise this, and think that it's the celebrities who have all the power.

We feel we have to check in with them on their channels,

news platforms, subscribe to their channels, and do Google searches to find out the latest. With the rise of 'fake news', there is no certainty as to whether what we're reading has any truth or validity, but we tune in nonetheless because we have become addicts. But there is something even more insidious at work. We're losing ourselves, the limited earth time we have is running out like sands in the hour glass. Our destinies - why we are on earth in the first place, is being sabotaged. Our self-esteem is going down the plug hole as we think that our lives are trifling and inconsequential compared to the lives of those we worship.

There are many magazines which come up with celebrity lists such as 'Forbes' Most Wealthy', 'People's Most Beautiful' or 'Glamour's Woman of the Year'. The fact that those in the running are limited to celebrities, show that the media is also under the spell of celebrity. Simply by virtue of being a celebrity, chances are you will appear on one list or the other. If it is indeed true that *"Great minds discuss ideas; average minds discuss events; small minds discuss people"* (attributed to Eleanor Roosevelt 1884-1962), then we have a culture of predominantly average and small minds.

It's important to recognise the false narrative for what it is – celebrities do not have a monopoly on all the attributes we rate highly in society whether it be intelligence, beauty, wealth or charm. It is illogical to think that only a select few famous people out of the entire world's population, have cornered the market on these attributes. We tend to think so little of ourselves that we can't bear to think that, like them, we too have what it takes to succeed.

It is commonplace to hear someone saying *"I love so and so ..."* – and more often than not, it is someone they have only seen or read about in the news but have never actually met. It would be more accurate to say, I love his/her music, acting method, artistry, style and similar expressions of admiration. It is technically impossible to love a person you have never met. True love involves suffering and sacrifice not just pining and emotional excitement. It would be more accurate to say that you admire something they have achieved.

A celebrity can morph into a 'brand' which seems to surpass being a mere mortal. This occurs when they venture into different fields of endeavour and cross over into different industries. They then assume an eponymous brand. For example, Gwen Stefani started off in a band where she came to public awareness, but now she is a solo singer, has started three fashion labels, and has appeared as a judge on 'The Voice' musical talent show. These celebrities then are famous for being famous in general not for any one feat or outstanding contribution in any one area. It may seem as if they have conquered the world and can do no wrong, that everything they touch turns to gold, but no achievement or reputation lasts forever; there will come a day when they too will be forgotten.

In the first two of the Ten Commandments, God warned His people not to have idols nor bow down before an *"... image, or any likeness of anything that is in heaven above, or that is in the earth beneath, or that is in the water under the earth."* (Exodus 20:4-5 NKJV) In modern times, our images have become more sophisticated. They are not carved or molten images which may be destroyed, stolen or degrade with time; they are digital and can be preserved long after the human beings whose images are digitally captured, have aged, had their appearance cosmetically enhanced or are dead. Idols separate us from God who is the power source who enables us to fulfil our life's purpose on earth, not just granting us access to eternity. He is the One who enables us to take our next breath – *"... in Him we live and move and have our being ..."* (Acts 17:28 NKJV)

Worship can never be divorced from life. Our entire life needs to be an act of worship. Idolising or worshipping celebrities can take over your life. They have a unique opportunity to affect peoples' minds. In press conferences and performances alike, they have the power to communicate resonant messages, and either glorify God or take all the glory for themselves.

Celebrity pre-occupation is blinding peoples' hearts to the real God, and feeding an unhealthy thirst for fame through entertainment shows such as X-Factor, 'American Idol' and 'The Voice'. Why this unhealthy need for fame? The average human being does not feel important because we know live in a culture where it has become acceptable to ignore the people around us, even those closest to us. We are so busy looking at our hand-held devices that we hardly notice one another anymore.

Similarly, we have become too lazy and absorbed with technology to take part in meaningful conversations with one another anymore. What's more, people have little or no sense of what they contribute to their work, families and communities since verbal compliments are few and far between. No emoticon or icon sent in a typed message can replace the emotional thrill of someone giving you a compliment face to face. We do ourselves no favours with the fact that our peer groups don't last for very long and keep changing. Yet, a daily rendezvous with your favourite Netflix TV episode can never substitute with spending time with friends and family. When the episode ends, nothing lasting will have been gained, but when you consistently invest in a friendship, you will reap a sense of mental well-being and potentially an enduring friendship.

Why do we assume celebrities hold the secrets to life in general? Just because they have distinguished themselves in one area or a few areas of their lives, the media saturates with information about all areas of their lives. Elizabeth Taylor, in her last interview (featured in Harper's Bazaar) said that *"... sometimes I think we know too much about our idols and that spoils the dream."*[27] Indeed, what is real to us can be different from what is actually real. Perhaps it is time we woke up from our culture-induced dream and realised that the clock is ticking, and it's time we start investing in our own dreams as opposed to dreaming about celebrities.

Chapter 8: The Neglected Self

What many fans may fail to recognise is that they are living vicariously through the celebrities they choose to follow. It is something we all do to an extent even if it is a brief thought of what it might be like to walk in someone else's shoes. It's useful and healthy to develop empathy for all types of people not just celebrities. Genuine empathy should lead to some form of positive action.

The significance of the individual has been sacrificed on the altar of celebrity 'idol' worship. Instead of people being taught to live their lives and discover their own destinies from the inside out through prayerfully seeking God's guidance, and inner reflection, they are fed the false values of hero worship which encourage them to loathe their own identities and instead crave to be like someone else. Mass hysteria is fuelled for a celebrity based on the most superficial of qualities such as beauty, popularity, or creative/performing ability. Behind it all is a strategic ploy by the media to maximise profits at the expense of peoples' wallets and their self-esteem.

Whilst we are busy 'fanning out' over the lives of others, there are many areas of our lives which are neglected. Apart from the more obvious mundane tasks such as housework, running errands, there are the personal tasks which only you can do for yourself. For example: Did you have enough exercise? Did you make sure you ate healthy balanced meals? Did you steal some quiet time to commune with your Creator and check in with yourself to make sure you are making strides towards the goals which really matter, and that you are generally happy with the way life is going? If you are wallowing in discontent, have you given some time to consider how you can make some changes to improve your situation? Popular culture will always seek to distract you from your life and divert attention away from yourself to other famous personalities we are programmed to believe deserve our unquestioning attention and adoration. If you do not summon up the will power to resist, you will be colluding in your own self-sabotage.

All these personal considerations take time, and consistent daily application to see your goals come to fruition. But most people do not prioritise themselves. It's very easy to lose yourself in celebrity addiction because, as these personalities loom larger and larger in your own mind, you get smaller and smaller. We may not even realise that we have fallen into this trap, due to a complex interplay of reasons.

Since childhood, you may have absorbed the narrative from trusted elders that you will not amount to anything, so why bother. Without realising it, you have chosen to believe these words, and they have become a self-fulfilling prophecy. You may also fail to realise that your relationship with yourself is your primary earthly relationship. After all, unless you are a 'Siamese twin' of sorts - you are the only one who is with you 24/7. You therefore need to give that relationship conscious effort, as you would a relationship with a best friend or significant other if you want it to thrive. Many are too lazy to do the work of building a life. In order to motivate yourself to stay fully engaged in building your life, you must first believe that you're worth it.

Some have assigned themselves to the category of 'losers', and others whom they follow so adoringly to the category of 'winners'. Such tags are not helpful as they seem to assign people to permanent categories, whereas *"... there's a time to gain and a time to lose."* (Ecclesiastes 3:6) Each life is a combination of failures and successes. Also, if you have convinced yourself that you're never going to win, why put in the effort to even try? Winning can be re-defined in terms of daily steps of progress towards your goals rather than a long-term, eventual outcome. Everything you do to improve and nurture yourself can be seen as a gain.

You may think your value lies in being noticed, so if no-one notices you, then you are no more than a nonentity. Pop culture encourages attention-seeking because it seems that everyone desires at least 15 minutes of fame, and the emergence of social media has made this possible. We have fallen for the flawed thinking that the more people pay attention to us, then the more our existence is validated. We fail to make a distinction between attention and love. People may love something you do or say but that doesn't mean they love you as a person.

You may fail to realise that the more you invest in yourself, the more you will then have to give to others. Also, your life will become more meaningful. The more meaning you derive from your own life, the less you will be tempted to spectate on other peoples' lives. By contrast, if you fail to invest in yourself, you will have little to offer the world, and your self-esteem will plummet accordingly.

Legitimate news has been blended with trivia to hijack our attention. We are now so bombarded with information that is usually graphically presented such that it is almost impossible for your brain to distinguish the two. We now know more about celebrities' private lives – breakups, engagements, birthdays, marriages, children – than we do about genuine geopolitical issues facing the world. The synthesis of celebrity and politics has been almost seamless. There is no better illustration of this than the increasing promotion of celebrities at political rallies prior to elections to stump for votes. We know that people are more likely to believe in the political views of a celebrity they esteem highly because they have already mindlessly submitted their wills to a celebrity if they have subscribed to their YouTube channel, follow them on Instagram or some other social media platform.

We all could benefit from asking ourselves - what is the

basis of our self-worth? There is now an obvious human divide between celebrities and 'unknowns'. The underlying message is that if your name or image is not out there, if people are not talking about you, if you're not listed in Wikipedia, have your book on a prominent bestseller list, such as NY Times, Amazon, or Sunday Times, have more than a certain number of hits on your webpage or YouTube videos, or other worldly indices of success, then you are worthless. In effect, your only worth then comes from being a follower and a watcher. Because this creates frustration, depression and self-loathing, there are some who are willing to do anything to become famous, even to the extent of committing a heinous crime, engaging in risky behaviour or making a fool of themselves.

A 2018 study revealed that between 2011 and 2017, 259 people died in pursuit of extreme selfies[28] . A couple, 29 and 30 years old respectively, recently fell to their deaths whilst taking a photo of themselves on a granite ledge with no railings in the Yosemite National Park in California[29]. They flirted with death for the temporary adrenaline rush of taking an extraordinary selfie, but they will never live to see how many 'likes' they would have gained on Instagram or other social media sites; nor will they be able to share with friends and family what it felt like to experience that moment before their tragic accident.

But there is another type of tragedy which unfolds silently and insidiously in the lives of those who consider themselves to be just average. Generally, they are resigned to just watching and following, and do not contribute anything unique or worthwhile – they simply buy and consume the products of others. Although this type of behaviour may yield initial excitement from, for example, talking about the latest blockbuster film, listening to the number one album on the billboard charts, or going to see the football club you support play in a famous arena, this soon wanes, and then it's back to your real life where you begin to anticipate and plan your next thrill-seeking activity. In all likelihood, nothing would have changed because you would not have invested any time or energy or resources into bringing about a positive change. You may even be oblivious to the fact that your life is slowly deteriorating – perhaps your friendships are becoming more distant, you are developing aches and pains in your body, and your marriage is on the verge of divorce.

We persist in feeding the baseless notion that other peoples' lives are more exciting than ours. Our suspicions are based overwhelmingly on pictures. We forget that pictures are tantalising and provocative but they also misconstrue reality. Truth can never be gleaned from a split-second click of the camera. We are unwitting members of the FOMO club (Fear of Missing Out) who always think 'the grass is greener on the other side', and others are having more fun or leading more fulfilled lives than we are. The irony is that we will continue to fuel this impression if we allow our celebrity addiction to persist unabated.

We human beings are very good at grading and categorising ourselves such that some are seen as more valuable than others; but we are all of equal value to God. Peter recognised this truth, *"... I perceive that God shows no partiality, but in every nation whoever fears Him and works righteousness is accepted by Him."* (Acts 10:34-35) There are things which God wants you to accomplish during your lifetime which only you can do in your own inimitable way.

On the face of it, what we do can be so similar; after all doctors, teachers, singers, cleaners all provide a service but it's the way each of us goes about the individual tasks, which set us apart as being unique. The 'where' and the 'when' also determine your unique assignment. You have been called to serve a unique constituency of people at a unique time in history, starting with your inner circles of those closest to you such as family and friends. If we take the uniqueness of our lives seriously enough, it has the power to transform us from dreamers to doers, from losers to winners, and from spectators to players. God has prepared unique work for each of us. (Ephesians 2:8-10)

It is possible that celebrities are also neglecting themselves because they too may be addicted to the hamster wheel of fame. Judy Garland stated in 1963 that the only time she felt wanted as a child was when she was on stage performing. Judy did not take to the life of a performer of her own accord, but was pushed into it by her stage-mum who insisted that Garland perform even when she was sick[30]. Although the world benefited from her talent, it came at a very high price – she died at 47 from an accidental drug overdose.

Indeed, if you're not doing what you're supposed to be doing, your heart will be empty even though you are busy, overtly productive and making lots of money. This may have been the case with Garland, and indeed many other stars who may stay in the 'fame game' because they feel obliged to do so. For starters, the livelihood of your family and employees may be at stake because many may have a stake in your reputation and brand.

It's easy to believe that we come into this world to do one thing and make a contribution in one area alone. It's a simplistic way of defining our destinies. No-one comes into the world to be an accountant, lawyer, salesman or cleaner. Rather our value comes from the service we give to others across a range of contexts, and our opportunities taken to help heal the world, ourselves and others.

Many celebrities end up pursuing another path besides the one which brought them to the media spotlight. They too can end up on unfulfilling paths which offer much but deliver little to soothe the longings of their souls. Because the careers of celebrities rely largely on public validation, it's easy for them to lose their identities in a sea of public opinion. Also, one career very often only lets us explore and develop one aspect of our personalities, or one divine calling when in fact there may be other callings to pursue down the track.

We neglect ourselves in other more subtle ways. Instead of having to think for ourselves, we are content to have imposed on us certain value judgements. Lifestyle and Culture-focused magazines are quick to publish lists such as 'The Ten Best Movies', 'Ten Best TV Shows', 'Ten Best Albums' of a particular year of in a performer's career, or a celebrities picks such as 'Oprah's Favourite Things'. Even subscribing to 'the Editors picks' of 'Books to Read', 'Places to Visit' and other similar compilations under the guise of bucket lists, means that we have allowed the opinion of a person we don't know, but who has the semblance of knowing best, to decide what direction our lives should take. The term 'Bucket lists' lends an urgency to reading and acting on these recommendations. Have we ever stopped to ask ourselves what really matters to us, so that we can formulate our own lists, and embark on our own personal journeys of discovery. It would be terrible to reach the end of your life, and realise that the pursuits in which you invested so much time and energy, or were directed towards by others, did not really matter in the end.

In the course of this personal adventure, you will probably stumble across things which are not popular or acclaimed but nevertheless appeal deeply to you. In athletics, there's such a term as 'personal best', and that is what we must seek to find. Enjoy what you come into contact with and experience in your daily life, rather than seek out what others rate. Seek to enjoy your own thoughts and imagination, and don't be ashamed to notice what and whom you're drawn to instinctively. Resist the constant tug to be drawn in a certain direction that the media wants you to gravitate toward - a subtle type of 'programming' which does not harness your highest potential. Be willing to let your life unfold organically so that you will have something unique and refreshingly different to offer the people in your world.

Chapter 9: Re-evaluating Success

F ailure and success cannot be properly assessed horizontally between individuals; it can only be properly assessed vertically in terms of divine calling which is unique to each individual. Silent introspection is needed over a prolonged period of time to discover this calling. Unfortunately, we often evaluate our success based on the trajectory of how others are doing, which either sets us up for feelings of envy or one-upmanship. We would benefit more from comparing how we were yesterday with how we are today, and the person we hope to be tomorrow. Henry David Thoreau, author of '*Where I lived and What I lived for*' (1924), writes, "*... the millions are awake enough for physical labour; but only one in a million is awake enough for effective intellectual exertion, only one in a hundred million to a poetic or divine life.*" Not everything an individual achieves will be admirable because every life is marked by failure as well as success.

Each of us, if given the chance and left to our own devices, would live life differently from each and every other individual who has ever and will ever live. Yet, this fact - too wonderful to be discounted - is often overlooked. The media has succeeded in seducing us into prescribed boxes or pigeon-holes on how we should live. Advertising has taught us how we should look, adorn our bodies as well as our houses, how we should spend our time and money. There is very little original thinking, much less living, and what little there is, is very soon replicated.

Without self-worth, you will have no incentive to invest in yourself. You will focus on these celebrity 'super-beings' whom the press have promoted as being icons of our culture and who are portrayed as having discovered the secrets of success. You may be deceived into thinking that the more you focus on them, the more you will learn how to succeed like them. But all true learning is pragmatic not theoretical. At some point, you will have to disengage from the media narrative to become pro-active on a personal level. In fact, you will discover that the more pro-active you become, the more your self-esteem begins to blossom, and the less desire you will have to remain updated on the latest celebrity gossip. In the process, you will be carving out your own success in your own unique way.

If we're too busy admiring others, we lose something of ourselves. We cannot be all we were meant to be if we have a copycat mentality. All of us, no matter how famous, beautiful, successful, clever, have an 'Achilles heel' and unattractive elements in our lives. We must start by being grateful for our own lives, and we can only do so by recognising our uniqueness and the positive contribution that we and we alone can make.

Fulfilling your calling will always seem an overwhelming feat. Because all true callings are of supernatural origin, they will require faith in God and his divine enablement to achieve them. God will never ask you to do something which you can accomplish in your own strength, as that would make Him redundant. Although dreams can appear daunting, it is re-assuring to know we do not have to rely on our strength and wisdom alone to bring them to fruition.

Why are we so bored with our lives? Could it be that we are so over-stimulated by the media portrayals of celebrities that our everyday lives seem lack-lustre by comparison. We can get more sensory stimulation from ten minutes of television than we would get in a whole day without TV – the background music, the intense array of colours, the different cast of characters paraded in quick succession – are in stark contrast to our real-time experiences when ordinarily we might interact meaningfully with a handful of people on any given day. Our perceptions have been dulled so that we no longer see the 'majestic' in the mundane. We take for granted the beauty all around us such as in Nature and the faces of the people we meet.

We do not find our real lives entertaining because the standard has been set unrealistically high. How can our ordinary lives compete with this 'High Definition', 'surround sound' assault on the senses? Although this has added to the stress on the human mind and body (so many allow technology to deprive them of much-needed sleep and genuine relaxation), we are happily hooked. It's like taking an amphetamine without even knowing it. In the UK, the Duke of Sussex, Prince Harry, has stated that *"Social media is more addictive than drugs and alcohol, and it's more dangerous because it's normalised and there are no restrictions to it..."*[31]

The sad fact is that the clock is ticking on your life in real time, and that some will only wake up from this distorted reality when they are dead. Your time on earth is limited, and you don't know how much or how little you have left. Age can be assessed in terms of the life we have remaining rather than the life we have already lived. Few know how much time is left, so we all need to live each day as if it were our last or among our last. It's often the case that only when some receive a prognosis of a terminal disease or other shocking news, or experience a devastating loss or trauma, that they will recognise the dire need to call time on their hero worship. If you are reading these words, it's not too late to wake up to the reality that your life does have significance after all, and that your calling awaits you at every turn. How will you respond?

Part 4: The Future

Chapter 10: Acknowledging the Illusion

Cameras click in staccato succession accompanied by flashing lights. There's nothing like the Red Carpet experience to convey the glitz and glamour of Hollywood. The danger is in thinking that this transitory walk down the Red Carpet where the attention of the whole world is on their shining faces, represents what it's really like to be a celebrity. The biggest illusion is spun by the impression that the minute-by-minute lives of celebrities is always as wonderful as the picture-perfect images we see in the media.

A society which overdoses on imagery is bound to promulgate half-truths because an image can be used to say whatever the user wants it to say. This fact is now exploited *ad nauseum* by the tabloids who have a tendency to invent a narrative based on a split-second photo. Therefore, instead of focusing on the product or talent associated with the celebrity, we have become more riveted by their personal dramas.

We all yearn for perfection or idealism in our own lives and if we give up on it for ourselves, we will seek it vicariously through others. We persist in feeding the baseless suspicion that other peoples' lives are more exciting than ours. Our suspicions are based overwhelmingly on pictures. We forget that pictures are provocative and tantalising but can never give the full truth. Truth can never be gleaned from a split-second click of the camera. Yet, all you need is one picture to send the imagination into overdrive.

Is it not part of the fantasy of fame that those who bask in its limelight, lead charmed lives? Therefore, when tragedies befall them, we somehow feel they will overcome and rebound the way a heroine does in a work of fiction. Even when their tragedies are played out in the full glare of the media, with or without their consent, we are lulled into a surreal sense that this is all part of the drama, and that sooner or later, they will bounce back. By imbuing them with this superhuman ability to overcome tragedies, we have divested them of true humanity. When there is no such recovery, we shower them with posthumous plaudits, concoct a conspiracy theory to explain away their demise or downfall, or we simply oust them from our memories by replacing them with another preferred 'celebrity of the moment'.

The illusion being spun is that being in the spotlight brings happiness, wealth, love – all you could wish for and more. Is it not the case that celebrity thrives on sanitised or carefully crafted media portrayals and 'self' portrayals. It is usually in the aftermath of their deaths that shocking and unsavoury truths come to light. Even if they or the lives they lead were as wonderful as they appear to be, it would still not justify the fact that we too readily relegate our lives to the back-burner whilst we bask in their reflected glory.

The Case of Liberace (1919-1987)

> *The American pianist, singer and actor was known for his flamboyance on stage, and his 'mega-watt' smile. It was not until his death in 1987 at the age of 67 that it came to light that he was homosexual. This lifestyle was very much frowned upon at the time, and he covered it up for fear of undermining his lucrative career. He even tried his best to prevent any post-mortem after his anticipated death following a protracted illness. It was to reveal that the cause of death was complications from AIDS[32].*

The last three generations from X, Y and Z have been the most greatly influenced by the media of the five generations that are still alive today, but in a way we have all become consumers and spectators. All the five generations have been exposed to some degree to the lure and appeal of entertainment-based technology, examples being the silent films and black and white television sets[33].

Celebrity overlaps every category of modern-day idol worship not just entertainment, and includes sports, religion, business, academia and politics. The famous are now being exposed in the most unflattering lights. Also, many achieve fame because of the horrible things they have done, not the admirable things. We seem to be drawn to the worst in others, and the worst in others is being exposed. Idolatry veils us from the read God, and casts us in a subservient role from which no lasting fulfilment can be found.

The models you see in the magazine do not look like that when they roll out of bed. If you happen to see any of the 'Ambush makeovers' on the Today Show in America[34], for example, it becomes obvious that the 'plainest of Janes' and the 'ugliest of Bettys' can be transformed into the most beautiful of swans. All it takes is a glam squad dedicated to making the best of their features. This leaves us under no illusion that someone else's features are no better than ours; rather it's a question of knowing or discovering how to make the best of the features we have.

It came as a shock when Luke Perry who had been dubbed a 'teen heart throb' from his career-defining role as Dylan McKay in 'Beverley Hills, 90210', suddenly died at the age of 52 from a stroke. By the time of his death, his good looks had faded revealing a man who looked 20 years older than his actual age[35]. Yet the 'heart-throb' image stuck throughout his life, lending credence to our tendency to believe familiar narratives we have been spun although they may no longer be true.

The illusion may seem static because we can watch re-runs of a TV series or films as often as we desire. The reality is more sobering. They too will age and die – sometimes prematurely and under tragic circumstances. But what about us – when do we get to live our dreams? Although celebrities die, we often resurrect them and sustain them on life support indefinitely. We continue to watch their films, listen to their back catalogue and, without realising it, we refer to them as if they are still alive. Some celebrities seem to have such a powerful hold on their fans that they worship them as much in death as when they were alive.

Digital efforts are underway to create more celebrity holograms so they can be digitally resurrected to perform on stage as if they were still alive. The technique involves projecting an image unto an angled piece of glass with a 3D effect, and is the ultimate in spinning illusions. This was achieved with Tupac Shakur at the 2012 Coachella Valley Music and Arts Festival despite the fact that he was murdered in 1996[36].

It's easy to lose sight of this wake-up call - whilst they may be gone, we're still here. Their lives may be over, but what will we do with the rest of our lives? There are endless amounts of beautiful and talented people, many in your own neighbourhood. Indeed, you might well be one of them. Except, no-one is singing their praises or yours. It's hard to believe in yourself when no one else does. But God has endowed you with amazing potential. Therefore, rejoice in who God made you to be even if you haven't yet become all you can be. The writer of Ecclesiastes wrote, *"... nothing is better for them [the sons of men] than to rejoice and to do good in their lives"* (Ecclesiastes 3:12) All those in the public spotlight have had their difficult moments of self-doubt or rejection. This is part of what it means to be human, but it's worth pursuing your dream regardless.

When you realise that you only have access to current information about someone if the media regards them as trendy or if they choose to send regular updates direct to their fan base. What this effectively means is that celebrities are not just controlled by the fan base, but they control the fans. When an appetite is not fed, it soon declines then dies. When you stop feeding your appetite for celebrity news, it will eventually diminish then die. This can be made easier by replacing you entertainment diet with a better 'food' source. Why not use the media to inform and educate yourself on a subject which will benefit yourself personally such as using a new language or skill?

On the flip side, celebrities can quite literally fall off the cliff edge of fame, never to be heard from again. This happened to Richard Simmons, the American fitness guru who was last photographed and interviewed by the media in 2014. However, it would be wrong to assume that he is dead or in danger. He may just have chosen to live his life in a more sane and calm reality where his life is his to live privately and not open for public dissection. Similarly, fans can choose to no longer participate in the cycle of adoration and addiction. It would be quite liberating to discover that life goes on for you and for them even though you no longer follow their every move.

Finally, there is no one way to live as a celebrity. We often think that celebrity is associated with a particular lifestyle, but the choice is ultimately down to the individual. For example, some celebrities are regularly seen out in public running errands without any bodyguards whilst others surround themselves with an entourage of security and other people on their team. There is therefore no such thing as a celebrity lifestyle. This is only the stereotype, namely that their lives are full of glamour, high-profile events, exotic holidays, and hob-nobbing with other celebrities. There are celebrities who contradict this stereotype and live reclusive lives. They show that it is possible to be a celebrity, and not necessarily live in the public spotlight. Ultimately, we are all in God's spotlight. His eyes may be compared to a camera lens - *"... there is no creature hidden from His sight, but all things are naked and open to the eyes of Him to whom we must give account."* (Hebrews 4:13)

Chapter 11: Reclaiming our Sanity

Albert Einstein, the famous theoretical physicist is credited with the statement *"... insanity is doing the same thing over and over again, but expecting different results"*. Those who hallucinate see things which are not real yet think they are real. It becomes more difficult to acknowledge that you are hallucinating, and need help if everyone around you also thinks that what they are seeing constitute reality. Since the dawn of the age of television, we have been experiencing a mass hallucination in the form of popular culture. From one screen which used to occupy pride of place in the centre of the living room – the focal point of family gatherings – has emerged a multi-headed monster comprising multiple screens of various technological devices whether mobile phones, laptops or otherwise. This means that our attention to our own lives is being hijacked at every turn.

Because we also do legitimate day-to-day functions on these screens such as pay bills, network with family and friends and programme satellite navigation to plot our travels, it's difficult to give up altogether our dependency on them. The challenge which we face is differentiating between the legitimate and illegitimate use of our time. The lure of seeing and knowing more is ever-present, so once we are on them, it's easy to be tempted to check the news, social media and browse online retailers who send us tantalising advertisements.

Social media has been identified as a major factor in the rise of depression and anxiety. Rather than simply focusing on the daily requirements and goals in our own lives, we are being bombarded with photos and information about other peoples' lives, whether close friends or celebrities. We can easily form a habit of comparing our lives with those whose portrayals of their own lives seem perfect, and far more enjoyable and fulfilling than ours. This then leads to a sense of inadequacy and envy. Instead of embracing the lives we have and making the best of them, we begin to despise them and conclude that we've been given a raw deal by God Himself.

Many have become casualties of the culture of the counterfeit where an image of reality is being promoted as the norm to which we should all aspire. They feel like failures and may take their own lives; they feel traumatised or frazzled, and seek refuge in antidepressants. They feel inadequate and indulge in escapism through mindless entertainment or narcotics and various other addictions. Why this persistent need to escape the demands of our everyday lives? By so doing, we are in effect wishing our lives away.

Facebook and Instagram are two prominent examples of social media where your popularity is likely to increase depending on how many photos you post on your accounts. It would be all too easy to upload a false identity using a profile picture of someone else. The messages uploaded on to your Facebook wall are available to all your countless numbers of 'friends' which means that you are not communicating in a meaningful way with anyone in particular. The fact that increasingly people are willing to risk their lives in pursuit of the ultimate selfie, confirms that our 'reality filters' have become skewed.

'Reality' is a common cultural buzz word; however, we must be careful not to equate it with truth. Whereas each person's neurological reality is unique because each person perceives and interprets reality in his or her own way, social reality is being engineered and social narratives spun which are being represented as truth. What if the life we see on TV, lived by fictional characters or edited versions of real people, is not life at all but a bogus representation of what reality is meant to be? What if we don't need more of the 'same ole, same ole' but something totally different which has the capacity, though seemingly small and simplistic, to satisfy our needs even more than all this media excess which only gives us a temporary sensation of fullness? There is something about the world with its empty promises and broken dreams which induces in us the need to let our imaginations run wild.

We cling to images of perfection and of idealism even if they relate only to the superficial such as our appearance. We need to recognise that these split-second snapshots of celebrities in various poses and postures, are not accurate portrayals of what's going on in their lives. Pictures can never tell the whole truth, and yet we are living in an-image based and image-driven society.

What's real is what's going on in your life at this very moment. Everything else is memory, hearsay or speculation. It is becoming the norm to live our lives vicariously through others. Most of the time, these 'others' are not even aware that we exist. But God knows that we exist and He knows where we are. He is calling out to us as He called out to Adam in the garden of Eden – *"... where are you?"* God knew perfectly well where Adam was, but Adam needed to recognise his need to draw close to God, confess his failings and be restored.

Celebrity scandals and world events can often seem more interesting and important than what's going on in our own lives. We live in the Information Age where we are bombarded all the time with more information than we can process or really need. It triggers the question – what information is really relevant to us? At every turn, we need to be asking ourselves – how will this inform me of what I need in order to improve my life? In a world which worships the famous, many describe themselves with the following epithets – *forgotten, insignificant, average, abandoned, rejected, inferior, a failure or just plain ordinary.*

Part of reclaiming our sanity is regaining the proper perspective. In God's eyes, each of us is extraordinary and unique, whether fêted by the world or not. We need to truly take on board that Jesus would have died to save you and me even if we were the last person in the world. Yet, there are celebrities whom the media have sacrilegiously labelled as "... more popular than Jesus Christ". This was a remark originally attributed to John Lennon, referring to the Beatles, in a 1966 interview which was first printed in the London Evening Standard[37]. Jesus posed the question - *"... what does it profit a man if he gains the whole world and loses his soul?"* (Mark 8:36) Your soul is the true essence of who you are; everything else we acquire in the world is merely transitory. Idol worship engenders passivity in our own lives. Accountability to God and others, fosters pro-activity.

Chapter 12: Re-evaluating Mentors

On becoming recognised, celebrities may suddenly become a presumed mentor to the countless thousands or millions of people they have never met. As if being a mentor to just one other person is not enough of a tall order, the famous often become unknowing and unwilling mentors to countless, impressionable people who hang on their every word. Celebrities may make 'off the cuff' remarks, and the next day may not even be able to recall exactly what was said in a press interview. Worse still, they may have said something in innocence which is totally taken out of context. To be misunderstood by one person is bad enough, but the sheer thought of being misunderstood by the masses, whether on a national or global scale, may cause immense anxiety and stress.

After a while, celebrities will grow weary of being idolised because, unlike us, they have a front row perspective on their worst selves. Elvis Presley famously said, *"... the image is one thing and the human being is another...it's very hard to live up to an image."*[38] They may wish to be regarded as human just like the rest of us, and perhaps that is why so many choose to write and publish tell-all, raw and unfiltered memoirs. They may go on talk shows to confess their addictions or medical diagnoses.

For the general public, it may be hard to imagine that they have unmet needs when they are portrayed as having everything – at least everything the culture values such as wealth, social status, and fame. However, they may lack the things which truly matter such as a solid spiritual foundation, true friendship, unconditional love, the affection and support of a family. They may be complicit in this portrayal because they have fallen prey to all the hype and begin to believe their own press. Sooner or later, the illusion will shatter.

But we need not wait for this illusion to shatter through

some tragic event in the life of our favourite celebrities. In reality we covet their lives because we despise our own. It is imperative that we discover what is good and admirable about our own lives, and if there is nothing we can identify, then realise that a life-transforming opportunity awaits us – *to start to develop at least one thing about ourselves that will impart the self-respect we so desperately need.* We need to fall in love with ourselves, and fall in love with the lives we have, rather than keep imagining what it would be like to live someone else's life.

Our imaginations are a powerful, God-given capacity to envision our future. It is this that will provide the fuel and impetus to strive towards the fulfilment of this vision. If we are constantly using our imagination to envisage the lives of others, then we are sabotaging this capacity and ultimately our own success. All we will have to look forward to is a life of frustration resulting from repressed desire and disappointment resulting from failed effort. Ultimately, this can lead to a deathbed of painful regret. But it doesn't have to be this way. Today is your day to wake up and move in a different direction – one step at a time - *"With God's power working in us, God can do much, much more than anything we can ask or imagine."* (Ephesians 3:20-21 NCV)

Celebrity is a disposable 'commodity'. The shelf life of most celebrities is very short. For the few who have a long shelf life, their days are still numbered. Every aspect of celebrities' lives is now regarded as fit to be in the spotlight, whether it be having children, getting married, getting divorced including the less seemly experiences such as overcoming addiction and recovering from abuse. There seems to be nothing that is considered too private to be exposed. Is it any wonder that celebrities are perceived as commodities who can be critiqued and discussed as if they have no human feelings. But we must remember that they are human, just as we are. Not only are celebrities not all they're cracked up to be, but celebrity itself is not all it's cracked up to be!

Human beings were never meant to be on pedestals, it does not matter how talented they are. Living in that rarefied atmosphere of constant adulation, inevitably leads to pride which then leads to self-destruction. Proverbial wisdom warns us that *"... pride goes before destruction..."* (Proverbs 16:18) Is it any wonder that so many celebrities end up destroying themselves by letting the warnings of danger from genuine friends fall on their deaf ears, and refusing to recognise their weaknesses for what they are.

Actually, we are all talented but some are better at harnessing their talents than others. Also, some gain stardom based more on who they know than their talents. Alternatively, they may have felt they had to grant a favour, however demeaning, to gain a favourable step up the career ladder. We should avoid envying others who appear to have made it, unless we are willing to pay the price they have paid. There are many who might confess, in hindsight, that the price was simply too high.

There is no way on earth that we can change who we are fundamentally. Any attempt to be someone we're not results in frustration and despair. The concept is asinine, the efforts futile. Nevertheless, over the course of our lives, we usually discover talents we never thought we had. *The clue to discovering hidden talent is looking at where your interests lie.* Also, we must always pursue goals which are meaningful to us, and when we do, our talents will rise to the surface to manifest our authentic selves. God does not burden people with talents which they have no inclination to use, but He may have a particular plan for them, for which they need the talent. The root meaning of 'enthusiasm' is divine inspiration. Not every talent that is developed will inevitably lead to fame, wealth or being in the public spotlight, but it will be of service to others in some way, and it will bring you the fulfilment you seek. Jesus provided the key to greatness when He affirmed that *"... the greatest among you must be a servant."* (Matthew 23:11 NLT) On the contrary, the popular wisdom is that the greatest amongst us has the most servants!

Furthermore, there is a dangerous trend that celebrities are being used to sell not just their creative products such as music, film, art, clothing brands, cosmetics and other lifestyle brands, but more insidious things like political views, healthcare choices and the like – things that really matter in the long run and in areas where they might not be the best qualified. Perhaps the best stance we can take is not to buy something just because a celebrity has endorsed it. To refuse to question another person's opinions or actions simply because of their celebrity status is to willingly surrender your own mind's ability to think for yourself This is a symptom of a cult mentality. Despite evidence of egregiously bad behaviour from a favoured celebrity, many die hard fans will still maintain their allegiances.

There's a lot of talk these days about finding the right mentor as being the key to success. There was a time when people were apprentices to learn a trade or there was someone in the workplace who was assigned to them to show them the ropes. Although there may be a lot of good advice on offer from mentors, you should never limit yourself to what your mentor achieved. The prophet Elisha closely followed his mentor, Elijah, until he was taken up into the clouds, desperate for an anointing of the double blessing. In the end, he exceeded Elijah's track record in many ways.

A mentor can provide helpful clues about how to go about something, but ultimately the decision must be yours, and you should not ignore your gut instincts. Whatever happened to learning from mentors in our families and neighbourhood communities? Mentors should emerge naturally from our community of neighbours, family and friends. Many have surrogate-mentors in the form of their favourite albeit distant celebrity who has no personal contact with them. Could it be that we are afraid of the demands and complications of real time accountability and face to face interactions? We struggle to engage in meaningful conversations with one another anymore, and as such we have little or no sense of what we contribute to our work, families and communities. Our peer groups don't last for very long and keep changing.

Who are the mentors in our lives? Do we know their character? Do we have relationships with them or are they 'idols' we peer at through screens who seem admirable from a distance? The recycled snapshots and videos we see of celebrities only represent a tiny percentage of their lives; the reality is that what we know about them, as they evolve from day to day, is practically zilch.

The reason a media role-model cannot ever be appropriate is because there is no relationship, no meaningful bond other than that between a star/idol and a fan, based on fantasy and illusion. The beautiful model or actress is not as beautiful as you think because much time, effort, cosmetics and photo editing goes in to achieving that image. The voice of that musician you admire is enhanced by instruments and clever arrangement. The sportswoman you idolise is not as strong or as skilled as you think – they rely on coaching, training and physiotherapy, even sports psychology – to keep them in peak form.

An individual can never be replicated. Why be a second-rate celebrity 'wannabe' when you can be a first-rate 'you'. You can replicate qualities such as hard-work, endurance, kindness, politeness. If you incorporate them into your character and lifestyle you will reap success in your life. We need to discern the positive, admirable traits of the famous people we are exposed to through the media or community, and what are the negative, unflattering traits to avoid.

Knowing and being able to form relationships with your role-models is key – that way they can play a conscious role in shaping your skills and attitudes. You may even discover that there are qualities they admire in you.

Chapter 13: Reconnecting to our Calling

The likelihood of our ever meeting a celebrity whom we admire is low; the probability of having a meaningful conversation is even lower, and the chance of developing a relationship with them is almost impossible. This begs the question of why we would devote so much time and energy to this elusive dream. Furthermore, why would we confer them with god-like status when their time on earth and in the spotlight, as radiant and intense as it may be, will not endure. Also, no human being's fame can be compared to God's fame which preceded mankind's very existence. He is known and will continue to be known by the angels, the planets and all of His creation, from eternity past until eternity future.

On the contrary, a lot of entertainment is futile because it stimulates the imagination but nothing fruitful results in our lives. We are kept glued to our seats by the special effects, the colourful, riveting backdrops, the fast pace of the plot which means we dare not look away for a second in case we miss something. Film industries worldwide spend millions of dollars on 'make-believe' re-enactments whether this be finding and customising exotic locations, creating and destroying sets, or designing realistic costumes; and the actors help to make it all seem so real by their convincing, realistic portrayals. By the time the credits roll, we feel as if we were there on the set ourselves and experienced the drama in real-time, but then the truth hits us – it was just 'make believe'. Life in the real world could only be escaped or postponed for so long!

It begs the question of why God gave us imaginations? We are meant to envisage the future which God has promised; then, strengthened by these inner images, we will be motivated to see them come to pass in reality. *Imagination should be used to create reality not to escape from it*. This is 'fertile' imagination because it yields positive fruits in our lives, and it empowers us to fulfil our life's purpose. 'Futile' imagination, on the other hand, leads to disappointment, emptiness and disillusionment.

Life is like one, big multi-screen TV. You can choose which channel to tune into. Choose wisely the channel which is most conducive to your destiny. King David pleaded to God to *"... turn my eyes away from looking at worthless things and revive me in Your way."* (Psalm 119:37)

We live in a modern world where we are bombarded by images. God warned His people against becoming fixated on images to the extent of it leading to idol worship and idolatry. The second Commandment states that, *"You must not make for yourself an idol of any kind or an image of anything in the heavens or on the earth or in the sea. You must not bow down to them or worship them ..."* (Exodus 20:4-5 NLT) Images have the capacity to deceive us. They can become so entrenched in our imaginations that they end up motivating us to desire the wrong things. God's desire is that we be led by truth not image. God's blueprint of how to think is found in the following admonition – *"Fix your thoughts on what is true, and honourable, and right, and pure, and lovely, and admirable. Think about things that are excellent and worthy of praise."* (Philippians 4:8, NLT)

The only way to discover our purpose is to re-commit to living a life which is rooted and grounded in reality and God's truth. Reality is what you are experiencing in the here and now which is not filtered through any other means than your body, mind and spirit. What's real is what's going on in your life at this very moment. God's truth is meant to guide and protect us by establishing moral boundaries for our lives.

One of the keys to disconnecting from celebrity mania is learning to live in the continuous present. We need to stop seeing and assessing the world through other peoples' lenses and filters. Instead of escaping from ourselves into screens, we can actively choose to spend our downtime away from screens and be fully conscious of the information coming to us through our five senses.

The ordinary moments of our lives all have extraordinary elements. Although our days may often seem like 'Groundhog Day' where we are repeating an endless number of mundane tasks, no day is experienced exactly the same. God gives us the re-assurance that our lives are meaningful by the fact that we are constantly at the forefront of His mind – *"How precious are your thoughts about me, O God. They cannot be numbered! I can't even count them; they outnumber the grains of sand!"* (Psalm 139:17–18 NLT). However, it's up to us to interpret our lives with as little or as much meaning as we choose. Yet, we are content to give more attention to the trivial aspects of the lives of celebrities than our relationship with the Creator.

Many of us have no idea what God's purpose is for our lives. It may never have occurred to us to simply ask Him. Yet, the assurance is for all - *"Keep on asking, and you will receive what you ask for. Keep on seeking, and you will find. Keep on knocking, and the door will be opened to you."* (Matthew 7:7 NLT)

Celebrity worship may yield a certain measure of excitement in the short term, but zero fulfilment in the long-term. It is the ultimate betrayal of yourself. The significance of the individual has been sacrificed on the altar of celebrity idol worship. Instead of people being taught to live their lives and discover their own destinies from the inside out through prayer, contemplation and self-examination, they are fed the false values of hero worship which encourage them to loathe their own identities and instead crave to be like someone else. So many miss their calling because they are too distracted by the clamour of the 'crowd' such that the still, quiet voice of God gets drowned out.

It's important to take the time to hear God speak. God speaks to us in different ways, and He knows how to get our attention, but often we may not know it is Him. When God called the prophet Samuel, he was just a boy under the mentorship of Eli, the priest. At first, he mistook God's voice for his mentor's, but when he learned to give God his full attention, God spoke to Him in a clear and discernible way:

> *"Samuel did not yet know the LORD because he had never had a message from the LORD before.*
>
> *So the LORD called a third time, and once more Samuel got up and went to Eli. 'Here I am. Did you call me?' Then Eli realised it was the LORD who was calling the boy. So he said to Samuel, 'Go and lie down again, and if someone calls again, say, - Speak, LORD, your servant is listening-' So Samuel went back to bed.*
>
> *And the LORD came and called as before, 'Samuel! Samuel!' And Samuel replied, 'Speak, your servant is listening.'"*

> (1 Samuel 3:7-10, NLT)

The problem is that most of us want to be living someone else's life – as we imagine it to be. If we really knew what it was like to live someone else's life, and to be in someone else's mind and body just for a day, we would recoil in shock. There is a price we all pay for being ourselves. It is a price we must be willing to pay to live the life we were meant to live, and that is the only life worth living.

To find your own path in life requires the courage to step aside from what the masses are doing, and to discover your own purpose. We must recognise that society will not always applaud or validate our choices. Many of us will be castigated or isolated for being too strange or unconventional. Your spirit longs to be free to soar and 'dance to the beat of your own drum', you must resist all attempts to keep it caged. The upside is that you will have left the company of the restless masses, and you will live with a deep sense of knowing that you are on the path of your destiny.

The validity of our dreams should not be determined by how famous we can become, but whether we can make a worthwhile contribution in some area or field of human endeavour. We cannot afford to follow pipe-dreams simply because we are dazzled at the achievements of others in the limelight.

Initially, in our search for our personal path, it may seem as if we are stumbling around in the dark. We long for the light, and it is tempting to settle for the counterfeit light of basking in someone else's reflected glory. A few of us may get the opportunity to share a celebrity spotlight, or associate with a celebrity for a brief period, but most will only access this spotlight through our imaginations. Yet, God has a spotlight on us at all times, and it is even more penetrating than any microscope, probing into areas we would rather keep hidden – *"... the LORD doesn't see things the way you see them. People judge by outward appearance, but the LORD looks at the heart."* (1 Samuel 16:7)

The question which must always be uppermost in our minds is whether we have done a good job with the divine assignments we are given. Sometimes doing a good job will result in our becoming famous but most of the time, it will not. One of the false values which have invaded mainstream thinking is valuing people on their net income or social media visibility and popularity. Jesus warned, *"How terrible when everyone says only good things about you..."* (Luke

6:26 NCV) He likened this to the fanfare that surrounded the false prophets whom the people welcomed because they told them what they wanted to hear rather than the truth. Seeking God and living His way will never be the popular path, but it is the only way to true freedom.

When we come into this life, we are to discover what God wants us to do. Becoming all that God created us to be is not as easy as it sounds, and will require inner work as well as outer striving. In a world where conformity is king 'becoming all you can be' is usually perceived as the quest. This usually involves charting your own course based on what you see others doing which appeals to you. But you have a unique place and purpose in the world, and blazing your own trail is always a daunting task. Nobody can tell you exactly how to go about it because it has never been done before. It will take faith in God as you take steps of faith.

However, you can breathe a sigh of relief because whether or not you fulfil your destiny is not all down to you. God's plan is that we seek Him and His will with our whole heart. He will then add His supernatural guidance and strength to our human efforts. God wants you to co-create your future with Him. On the contrary, celebrity worship will deprive you of your future because it will take and take from you – time, self-esteem and financial resources – but never give back anything of any lasting value.

We are victims of the way we see ourselves, not the way the world sees us. In the modern world, we are encouraged to be so hard on ourselves because we are constantly baited into comparing ourselves with others because we are bombarded by images and information about others which portray their lives as being ideal, or better than ours. We have a tendency to criticise the way we look, envy others and give up on our dreams. Niggling doubts may creep into our minds that maybe we are inferior to others, and we may blame God for making us inferior. But, as Eleanor Roosevelt once said, *"no-one can make you inferior without your consent."*

Your relationship with yourself in terms of what you think and say about yourself, is fundamental to your happiness because it is what you tell yourself that will permeate your sub-conscious mind and determine your behaviour. Why be your own worst enemy? It is worthwhile to get into the habit of dismissing negative thoughts and counteracting them with positive thoughts the moment we open our eyes each day and come into full consciousness. This is a critical moment which sets the tone for the entire day and whether it will be one of courage or defeatism, mindful endeavour or mindless escapism.

Think of your life in terms of every decision you make having huge ramifications for the future because it does. You have life-affirming decisions to make each day to reclaim your destiny and avoid the celebrity bandwagon.

- o Instead of feeding the habit of following celebrities on social media or the like, schedule your day to focus exclusively on what is going on in your natural environs.

- o Aim to stay in the moment. With practice you will get better at staying focused.

- o The Hollywood dream is probably not your dream. So what is your dream?

- o Have the courage to write your own script, rather than be distracted by the dramas of others. Be the star in your own life.

- o Use your imagination, not to escape reality, but to 'pre-play' the future of your dreams.

o   When you find yourself fixating on celebrities, ask yourself *"What am I avoiding in my own life?"*

o   Each day or week, aim to take a reality check to ensure you are pursuing goals which are meaningful to you, and make the best use of your talents and skills.

o   Pay attention to your 'self-talk', feelings and fears. They are all messages and clues to destiny.

o   What you perceive as your desire for fame, may simply be a desire for 'self-validation' which comes from making it in this world on your own terms, rather than just seeking to be a carbon copy of someone else.

o   Notice the details, see the signs and be alert to the opportunities that come your way.

o   Resist the lure of escaping into fantasy, or getting high on the various addictive substances dished up by the popular culture.

Your future need not be a continuation of the past. You have read this book so now you are wise to the pit falls of celebrity worship. Instead of being awestruck by celebrities, let us rather seek to improve some aspect of ourselves. We can then celebrate our progress in a meaningful way.

Afterword: Lessons from Lockdown

Our appetite for celebrity news is no longer being stimulated the way it was prior to the arrival of the 2020 Covid-19 'pandemic'. Suddenly we were forced to recon with issues of life and death, physical and mental health and economic survival this social crisis places us at the crossroads. We must ask ourselves whether we will continue to fixate on celebrities of focus our limited time and energy on mediating this crisis. People were furloughed or lost their jobs as businesses closed, some for good. Even with the rent and mortgage moratoriums, this was only putting off the inevitable and other bills still needed to be paid. In the entertainment world, theatres and cinemas were forced to close and the release dates of films such as the latest James Bond movie were postponed.

The news assaulted us day by day, hour by hour, minute by minute with sobering, sometimes frightening statistics of those succumbing to the corona virus. Suddenly we came face to face with our own mortality, and that of our loved ones leaving us with the uneasy feeling that we could fall prey to this virulent disease at any time. To make matters worse, we might be asymptomatic carriers and pass it on unknowingly. All this fear and uncertainty made us retreat into our homes and safe spaces at a safe distance from others.

Although many of us had more time on our hands at home, exiled from offices and the third spaces we used to frequent such as restaurants and pubs, we were prone to foraging for the latest news about the corona virus:

- o What was the daily update from the government?

- o How many had succumbed in the area where we lived?

- o What places had re-opened and what remained shop?

- o What was the latest emergency item that was being cleared off the shelves? Was it toilet paper, disinfectant wipes or eggs?

- o What tier had our governments put is in this week, and how would that impact our movements?

Was there any inclination to check on:

- o Gwen Stefani's latest outfit,

- o Whether rumours of Kim and Kanye's divorce were true,

- o How many weeks at number one was Mariah's classic Christmas song,

- o What was Tom Cruise's latest blockbuster?

Covid did us all a favour by becoming the great equaliser. Suddenly, our lives were no longer ordinary and the lives of celebrities extraordinary. We had all collided simultaneously with an extraordinary set of circumstances over which we had no control. Navigating the terrain of our lives each day mentally and physically became an ever-present challenge. We read breaking news which made it crystal clear that we were all equal:

- o Celebrities were being diagnosed with Covid-19.

- o Celebrities were having to socially distance from their families.

- o Celebrities were losing work and income.

We should never rejoice in the suffering of our fellow

human beings no matter their status. But hopefully this woke many up to the fact that their perceived 'gilded cages' could not safeguard them from such reversals of fortune and tragedy. Like the ordinary folk, they were starved of publicity, so they took to YouTube to generate their own publicity. But what did they have to offer us which would satisfy our yearnings for safety, reassurance and a return to normalcy? With no new product to peddle – whether music, film, show, book or fashion line, they suddenly lost their sparkle. Even if they did, would we be so quick to sacrifice our precious income on 'non-essential' items when job insecurity was on the rise.

Suddenly every penny counted for things which mattered – really mattered. We were reading daily of the increased demand for food banks and that families were going hungry because children were no longer accessible to free school dinners due to prolonged school closures. This just wasn't happening to poor families, the middle class were having to swallow their pride and seek such assistance as well.

But even when this pandemic is finally over, there will always be the temptation to navigate the mouse in the direction of a scintillating headline about a celebrity's private life. Hopefully, my mind will press the pause button in protest, *"wait, stop, that's not legitimate newsworthy of my time and attention!"* After all, are celebrities posing on a beach on holiday really news? This happens to me time and time again. The traps will always be there, but I have learned to be more discerning and discriminating. In such instances, we have the opportunity to 'vote with our fingers', by either clicking away or clicking off! The acid test is always the same – does it really matter? Will it matter a year, five or ten years from now? As I grow older, I can no longer avoid the truth that my time on earth is limited. So, I might as well strive to do something worthwhile with the life and time which remains, rather than just dwell on these 'glorified' others whom the media have elevated to godlike status.

Perhaps, like me, it's when you feel most demoralised, exhausted or discouraged that you are most inclined to grab a brief hiatus from your own life with all its problems, and have a 'nosey' into someone else's. Soap operas used to be the go-to form of escapism, until the actors' personal lives became the focus of the media attention. This was a clever ploy by the media to ensure we were hooked every second of the day and not just during the televising of each episode. But we do not need to be the lab rats in this cultural experiment to hijack our minds. A mind is a terrible thing to waste, and we can best use our minds for other more meaningful activities such as praying, planning, and being pro-active. Imagination is meant to be used to create reality, not escape from it.

Conclusion

The future is bright if we are willing to reclaim it. It has always been the case that if we are not courageous enough to write our own life scripts, someone will write them for us. We will need to be more self aware, and be ever vigilant of when third parties are overwriting ours. Most of what we know, and think we know about celebrities, is mediated through third parties. Because we don't know them personally, we rely on sporadic images, headlines and captions to create a narrative which is a hodgepodge at best. Even the photos and information they share about themselves is bound to be selective, and carefully weighed to preserve the image they want to perpetuate in the public imagination.

Just as we now have digital devices such as 'fitbits' to monitor all aspects of our physical health, we need to find ways of staying alert to the psycho-spiritual dangers of celebrity idol worship. We need to guard against minimising or dismissing their flaws and magnifying their strengths. This will only lead to a skewed perception of them. We end up idealising their lives and idolising them. It is also reasonable to conclude that most of their flaws are hidden, as is the case with most human beings. It is only through face to face, direct and unfiltered interaction with them over a significant period of time, that you would ever become aware of their flaws and fallibilities. With the exception of close family members and very close friends, most of us will never be allowed such access. And why would we even want to; we have enough on our plates dealing with our own lives.

A key to breakthrough is to explore your areas of interest independently of what or who is topical in the current news cycle. You may discover that you enjoy the music of musicians who never came to fame, or artists who did not win awards, and poets who never gained the national spotlight, or actors who feature in obscure films but deliver unforgettable performances. It's important to widen your net so you don't fixate on one or only a few who are the 'media darlings' of the day.

Those of us who have a tendency to latch on to idols need to re-direct the lens back on to ourselves. It can be depressing to take a hard look at ourselves and our lives. There's usually a reason for this subtle form of self-avoidance. Working on ourselves means having to acknowledge that we've failed or messed up, and the uphill climb to the 'promised land' may seem too steep. It's so much easier to live vicariously through the achievements of others. Secretly, however, self-esteem plummets to the degree that celebrity fixation intensifies. Deep down, you will know you are betraying yourself.

The possibility awaits us of showing up and starring in our own lives. If we keep running for cover by escaping into celebrity news when the pressures of life hit, we will never realise how strong we can be. There are countless opportunities to celebrate the incremental progress we make, and the personal milestones we reach. We can each move to the beat of our own peculiar drum.

Don't let the culture decide your habits. You decide who you will celebrate, what you will let in your eyes and ears. Culture is about mind control and its chief tool is the media, but it also relies on materialism and commercialism which is based on the desire to be like others and to have what they have; as well as the psychology of the herd instinct.

It all boils down to who or what do you love. The culture promotes the love of money, the idolising of celebrities and fame. The media machine is so relentless that it can take over your entire mind and life. Worship can never be divorced from life. Our entire life needs to be an act of worship reserved for the true living God. Fanning out over celebrities or hero-worship of them can take over your life. This will be impossible if we focus on loving God with *"... our whole mind, body, soul and strength."* If we love God, we will strive to do what He says.

Celebrities have a unique opportunity to affect peoples' minds. In press conferences and performances alike, they have the power to communicate resonant messages, and either glorify God or otherwise. Celebrity worship is blinding peoples' hearts to the real God, and feeding an unhealthy thirst for fame. But our focus must not be on gaining fame but rather God's approval, and self-respect.

The fame of celebrities is mainly linked to the film industry, the music industry or the fashion world. These industries are based on false values such as *"... the love of money* [materialism and marketing], *the lust of the eyes* [image and glamour], *the lusts of the flesh* [sexual fantasy and promiscuity]" (1 John 2:15). Don't live your life in such a way that God only gets the left-overs. Pay attention to these cautionary words:

> *"If you love the world, the love of the Father is not in you. All that is in the world – the lust of the eyes, the lust of the flesh and the pride of life, is not of the Father."*

> *(1 John 2:15-16)*

Rather, determine to *"seek first the kingdom of God and His righteousness"* (Matthew 6:33). Determine to get rid of the false gods of pop culture and the idols in your heart so you can give God your whole heart.

The focus must be re-directed from the famous or 'when will I be famous' to the challenge presented by this book – the pursuit of self-intimacy and your divine calling. The cacophony of competing noises must be tuned out to enable you to hear the voice of your destiny – God calling you to be all you were meant to be. When all is said and done, the ultimate achievement is for God to say *"well done!"* Whose smile and nod of approval will have the most positive and lasting effect? The One who created you and scripted your calling will surely have the last word. The only way to discover this calling is to seek your Creator. Your calling may not be applauded in this world and it may not make you famous, but in its fulfilment you will find your own fulfilment and your life will have made a difference.

End Notes

1. [https://goodnessofgodministries.international/2011/05/21/the-god-of-entertainment-an-idol-that-is-consuming-america/, accessed April 3, 2019

2. 'What Makes a Good Life? Lessons from the Longest study on Happiness, Robert Waldinger https://www.youtube.com/results?search_query=TED+What+makes+a+good+life%3F+Lessons+from+the+longest+study+on+happiness, accessed 20 December 2018

3. https://www.telegraph.co.uk/news/newstopics/howaboutthat/11014591/One-in-five-children-just-want-to-be-rich-when-they-grow-up.html, accessed 13 March, 2019

4. Ref: the litmus test of spiritual purity – Culture Detox: Cleansing our minds from toxic thinking, p.13

5. https://en.oxforddictionaries.com/definition/fantasy accessed April 26, 2019

6. http://www.cracked.com/blog/5-destructive-sides-celebrity-culture-no-one-talks-about/ by Kathy Benjamin, accessed January 18, 2019

7. 'Youtube: 'The final 24 – Anna Nicole Smith'

8. https://www.theguardian.com/film/2018/oct/25/the-untold-story-of-lost-star-river-phoenix-25-years-after-his-death accessed December 22,2018

9. www.forbes.com, accessed January 31, 2019

10. https://people.com/celebrity/celebrities-who-love-or-hate-fame/ (accessed December 31,2019

11. https://www.businessinsider.com/what-age-are-

people-happiest-2017-12?r=US&IR=T, accessed 4 February 2019

12. https://www.elle.com/culture/celebrities/news/g30279/leonardo-dicaprio-kate-winslets-friendship/ accessed April 30, 2019

13. https://www.hellomagazine.com/celebrities/2018080260808/jennifer-aniston-fertility-struggle-candid-interview/ accessed December 18, 2018

14. https://inews.co.uk/opinion/columnists/david-beckham-marriage-hard-work/

15. https://www.psychologytoday.com/us/blog/counseling-keys/201702/nine-types-love, accessed 5 February 2019

16. https://www.thedailybeast.com/how-jackie-kennedy-invented-the-camelot-legend-after-jfks-death, accessed 17 December 2019

17. https://www.theguardian.com/tv-and-radio/2019/mar/04/the-michael-jackson-accusers-the-abuse-didnt-feel-strange-because-he-was-like-a-god accessed March 10, 2019

18. https://variety.com/2018/music/news/demi-lovato-concert-canceled-hospital-overdose-1202883262/, accessed 4 February 2019

19. https://www.her.ie/music/justin-bieber-opens-up-about-struggling-with-fame-264682 accessed April 30, 2019

20. Alice Robb, "The Four stages of Fame: How celebrities learn to accept and regret their popularity, www.newrepublic.com, accessed January 16, 2019

21. https://www.vanityfair.com/hollywood/2017/03/feud-joan-crawford, accessed 19 January 2019

22. https://www.independent.co.uk/news/people/jennifer-lopez-faces-backlash-for-using-all-lives-matter-phrase-on-twitter-a7133996.html, (accessed December 16, 2018

23. https://www.billboard.com/articles/columns/pop/8485998/mariah-carey-colin-kaepernick-photo-reactions Accessed December 16, 2018

24. https://www.buzzfeed.com/ryanschocket2/hailey-baldwin-has-responded-to-people-saying-justin-bieber accessed April 30, 2019

25. https://www.thelist.com/112485/tragic-real-life-story-judy-garland/ accessed February 5, 2019

26. https://newrepublic.com/article/116227/celebrity-study-four-phases-accepting-fame accessed March 13, 2019

27. https://www.harpersbazaar.com/celebrity/latest/news/a676/kim-kardashian-elizabeth-taylor-interview-0311/ accessed December 20, 2018

28. https://www.bbc.co.uk/news/newsbeat-45745982 accessed November 9, 2018

29. https://www.theguardian.com/environment/2018/oct/30/yosemite-deaths-couple-selfie-vishnu-viswanath-meenakshi-moorthy accessed November 9, 2018

30. https://www.biography.com/news/judy-garland-facts-bio accessed April 30, 2019

31. https://www.harpersbazaar.com/uk/culture/

culture-news/a27038789/prince-harry-social-media-more-addictive-alcohol-drugs/ accessed April 30, 2019

32. documentary film 'Liberace: Behind the music' 1988

33. https://blog.scienceandmediamuseum.org.uk/the-decline-of-black-and-white-tv/ accessed May 30, 2019

34. https://www.today.com/style/more/ambush-makeover/ accessed May 30, 2019

35. I newspaper, 'Perry's Death is a reality check for my teenage self' by Siobhán Norton, p.17, 7 March 2019

36. https://theundefeated.com/features/the-strange-legacy-of-tupacs-hologram-after-coachella/ accessed May 31, 2019

37. https://www.rollingstone.com/music/music-features/when-john-lennons-more-popular-than-jesus-controversy-turned-ugly-106430/ accessed April 30, 2019.

38. Elvis Culture: Fans, Faith, & Image 1999) by Erika Lee Doss, p. 218

Also by the Author

Available from jesusjoypublishing.co.uk

Dr Carla's Books and Blogs

www.culturedetox.net & www.sinavo.org

Culture Detox

Celebrity culture has burgeoned to almost breaking point, threatening to hijack our minds to absorption with the trivial and the pointless.

How did we get to a point when we know more about a celebrity than our own grandmother?

World events of great significance have been relegated to fine print to make room for scandal-mongering headlines. Consumers of news struggle to discern between relevant news and celebrity gossip and speculation. As a result, the media have whet the public appetite for non-stop entertainment and a desire for fame.

In her book, Culture Detox, Dr. Carla Cornelius urges us to step aside from this cultural madness, long enough to recognise it for the hollow, distorted reality that it is. Unfortunately a simple sip of green tea will not suffice to rid our minds of the toxic thinking to which we have become addicted. Carla examines the roots of our cultural malaise and offers us guidelines on de-junking our minds from the false values of our modern age.

ISBN: 9781907971006

Captive Daughters

At a time when so many advocates and activists are lobbying for the enforcement of women's rights and trying to improve their socio-economic status across the globe, it would be all too easy for the emotional and spiritual needs of women to be side-lined. Despite the modern woman's political and educational gains, she still battles certain life-limiting tendencies. Many women are still captive to:

The beauty myth which stems from the misconception that improving their appearance will transform their lives from the outside in, or the belief that their value is determined by how they look.

Choosing inappropriate female role models usually from the glossy industries of entertainment and fashion where style is valued over substance.

Romantic delusions spun by the Hollywood industry where the focus is on 'boy meets girl' then they live happily ever after with no real understanding of what it takes to stay married.

Trying frenetically to juggle the myriad roles they undertake while still finding time to nurture their own souls and maintain physical health and well-being.

These are some of the major challenges women face which represent chains which hold them captive. These chains can only be broken by having the courage to tackle long-held mind-sets and savouring the freedom only to be found in truth-centred thinking.

ISBN: 9781907971037

No Way Out

'No Way Out' is a psycho-spiritual appeal to hurting humanity in the hopes of preventing tragic deaths by suicide. It speaks directly to the hearts of the individuals who are ultimately in charge of their own lives and have the power to decide whether to live or die. It makes a compassionate appeal to those individuals to choose life whilst providing soul-searching keys to breaking free from suicidal tendencies.

Through a mix of study and reflective exercises the reader is guided to finding this capacity to take charge of their own lives.

It makes an ideal, anonymous gift to someone you suspect

may be depressed or suicidal since the subject of suicide is still a difficult one to broach. By so doing, you can intervene without invading privacy or causing further distress.

Dr Carla is director of the SINAVO Project [Suicide Is Not A Viable Option].

ISBN: 9781907971457